Black Writers and the Hispanic Canon

Twayne's World Authors Series

David William Foster, Editor

Arizona State University

TWAS 867

NANCY MOREJÓN
Photograph by Mel Rosenthal. All rights reserved.

Black Writers and the Hispanic Canon

Richard Jackson

Carleton University

Twayne Publishers
An Imprint of Simon & Schuster Macmillan
New York

Prentice Hall International
London • Mexico City • New Delhi • Singapore • Sydney • Toronto

Twayne's World Authors Series No. 867

Black Writers and the Hispanic Canon
Richard Jackson

Twayne Publishers
An Imprint of Simon & Schuster Macmillan
1633 Broadway
New York, NY 10019

Library of Congress Cataloging-in-Publication Data

Jackson, Richard L., 1937–
  Black writers and the Hispanic canon / Richard Jackson.
      p. cm. — (Twayne's world authors series ; 867)
    Includes bibliographical references (p.   ) and index.
    ISBN 0-8057-7801-2 (alk. paper)
    1. Spanish American literature—Black authors—History and
  criticism.   2. Blacks in literature.   3. Best books—Latin America.
  4. Canon (Literature)   I. Title.   II. Series: Twayne's world
  authors series ; TWAS 867.
PQ7081.J2635   1997
860.9'89608—dc21   97-6682
                                                                          CIP

To D.D., Shaw, and Charley, in memory of Lil and Chris

Contents

Voices previously drowned out . . . can have special meaning in the struggle to eradicate inequality.

Allan Hutchinson

Preface

Almost 30 years ago I published "An Underdeveloped Area" (*Hispania* 48 [December 1965]: 870), a complaint about how Black Hispanic literature had been overlooked by critics. Judging by the many books on the subject that have appeared over the past several years, this is no longer the case. Black Hispanic authors themselves, however, are still not widely represented in the Hispanic canon. This book proposes their inclusion. In another earlier publication ("Literary Blackness and Literary Americanism: Toward an Afro-Model for Latin American Literature," *Afro-Hispanic Review* 1, no. 2 [1982]: 5–11), I argued that many Black Hispanic writers can easily be classified or identified as excelling, for example, as Romanticists, Realists, Naturalists, *Modernistas,* or representatives of the "new novel" in Latin America. I now extend those remarks, later published in my book *Black Literature and Humanism in Latin America* (Athens: University of Georgia Press, 1988), beyond considering Black literature as texts that represent movements and trends. My primary objective in this work is to identify essential Black Hispanic authors whose works should be better known and can represent the Hispanic canon itself.

Those authors whom I believe merit consideration are Juan Francisco Manzano, Cuba's slave poet; Nicolás Guillén, Cuba's National Poet; Pilar Barrios, the dean of Black writers in Uruguay; Juan Pablo Sojo, author of the first Black novel in Venezuela; Adalberto Ortiz, whose work *Juyungo,* is the classic Black Ecuadorian novel of the 1940s; the Afro-Peruvian *decimista* Nicomedes Santa Cruz; the Afro-Colombian Manuel Zapata Olivella, one of the most prolific Black authors writing in Spanish over the last 50 years; and Cuba's Nancy Morejón, already one of today's best-known Afro-Hispanic authors in Black, feminist, and Third World circles. I also include Nelson Estupiñán Bass, an Afro-Ecuadorian compatriot of Ortiz with a creative output that rivals Zapata Olivella's in size; the Dominicans Blas Jiménez and Norberto James, two new Black Hispanic writers already familiar to Afro-Hispanists in the United States; Antonio Acosta Márquez, a new Venezuelan Black poet; the Afro-Panamanians Carlos Guillermo Wilson, known as Cubena, and Gerardo Maloney; and their Central American colleague, the Afro–Costa Rican Quince Duncan. Ian Smart, a leading authority on Central American literature, considers Duncan to be Costa Rica's most important living writer and Carlos Guillermo Wilson to be one of Panama's major living writers.

All 15 of these key writers, in fact, are well known to Afro-Hispanists and some—Nicolás Guillén, especially—to a more general readership as well. Taken together, they have written a great deal, but I limit my comments, for the most part, to such defining texts as Manzano's *Autobiografía* [*autobiography*], Guillén's early work *Motivos de son* [Son *Motifs*] as well as his much later *El diario que a diario* [*The Daily Daily*], and Morejón's "Mujer negra" ["Black Woman"], widely considered to be her most important poem, in Cuba; Juan Pablo Sojo's *Nochebuena negra* [*Black St. John's Eve*] and Antonio Acosta Márquez's *Yo pienso aquí donde . . . estoy* [*I Think Right Here . . . Where I Am*] in Venezuela; Pilar Barrios's *Piel negra* [*Black Skin*] in Uruguay; Ortiz's *Juyungo* and Estupiñán Bass's *El último río* [*Pastrana's Last River*] in Ecuador; Nicomedes Santa Cruz's *Ritmos negros del Perú* [*Black Rhythms of Peru*] in Peru; Manuel Zapata Olivella's *Chambacú, corral de negros* [*Chambacú, Black Slum*], *Changó, el gran putas* [*Changó, The Bad Son of a Bitch*], and *¡Levántate mulato!* [*Mulatto, Arise!*] in Colombia; Cubena's *Los nietos de Felicidad Dolores* [*The Grandchildren of Felicidad Dolores*] and Gerardo Maloney's *Juega vivo* [*Get Hip*] in Panama; Quince Duncan's *Los cuatro espejos* [*The Four Mirrors*] in Costa Rica; and Blas Jiménez's *Caribe africano en despertar* [*African Caribbean Awakening*] and Norberto James's *Sobre la marcha* [*On the Move*] in the Dominican Republic.

I could incorporate additional names and titles into this list, because it should be expansive. For example, in Colombia alone the nineteenth-century poet Candelario Obeso and his twentieth-century colleagues Arnoldo Palacios and Jorge Artel, who died in 1994, certainly merit consideration as do, for example, Aida Cartagena Portalatín in the Dominican Republic and Marcelino Arozarena, the subject of a special future issue of the *Afro-Hispanic Review,* in Cuba. Their key writings (as well as the works that I do discuss) could fit nicely in a parallel survey course on Black Hispanic authors or be integrated in or interspersed over a variety of standard courses and reading lists in academic Spanish departments. They could also be incorporated into the standard humanities curriculum, especially because several of these titles are now available in English. I cite from some of these translations in this study, although unless otherwise noted, all translations are my own.

I approach my critical readings from angles that in some instances differ from previous interpretations, including some of my own and even the authors' as well. The meaning I ascribe to these texts illustrates how Black Hispanic writers have had to confront not only the same obstacles that Blacks encounter in the United States but others as well that are peculiar to Latin America. Although these authors employ different approaches in their works, which account for the occasional comparisons I make, rarely do their characters function, experience, or do anything independently of race and color. This is true as much in the literature of the Afro-Cubans I discuss in chapter 3 as in that of the other Afro-Hispanic writers whom I discuss in the rest of the book. As for a personal theoretical framework, I would have to say, paraphrasing Gustavo Pérez Firmat ("My Critical Condition," *Latin American Literary Review* 20, no. 40 [1993]), that I have none. I am not concerned with signifiers and signifieds or, I would add, with theoretical manifestos. Rather than getting lured into the "unseemly scramble" for a theory (Anibal González, "The Lure of Theory in Contemporary Latin American Literary Criticism," *Revista de estudios hispánicos* 27, no. 2 [1993]: 291), I am only concerned, as in my previous work, with what Hispanic literature—and in particular, Black Hispanic literature—tells us about Blacks, about how we should treat others, and about how it can help us live our lives.

Although I have no theory, I do have premises. First, a variety of writers reflects the heterogeneity of Latin America better than do a chosen few because different authors bring different insights and perspectives to their work, and this multiplicity allows for a more comprehensive vision of reality. Second, we as literary critics cannot avoid the race issue, especially when Black Hispanic writers themselves are still writing about it. Whether they express themselves by means of autobiographical statements, fictional characterizations, or poetic personae, how these authors resolve the race issue is part of what makes these works worth reading. Third, race (Blackness) in Latin America should be looked at from a Black North American perspective because Black Hispanic writers do it themselves in their literature. Fourth and finally, Blackness enriches not only Black literature, the Hispanic canon, and the "White" literary movements and forms that that canon represents but also the whole debate on diversity now gaining currency in the United States. Black Hispanic authors write to combat invisibility in their homelands. We should not ignore them in ours or in our classrooms.

Acknowledgments

I would like to thank both my university for years of support and recognition and the Twayne editors for taking an interest in studies like this one.

Chronology

rights to such children born of non-Hispanic immigrants of African ancestry.

1942   Ortiz's *Juyungo* wins first prize for novels in the Ecuadorian Concurso Nacional.

1943   Ortiz publishes *Juyungo*, Ecuador's first Black novel.

Sojo publishes *Nochebuena negra*.

1947   Zapata Olivella's first visit to the United States. Meets Langston Hughes in Harlem.

1962   Zapata Olivella's *Corral de negros* awarded Casa de las Américas literary prize in Cuba.

1966   First edition of Estupiñán Bass's *El último río*, which he later revised and abridged.

1969   Norberto James's poem "Los inmigrantes" wins a prestigious literary prize from the University of Santo Domingo.

1975   Carlos Guillermo Wilson completes Ph.D. in Spanish at UCLA.

Nancy Morejón's "Mujer negra" first appears in *Casa de las Américas*.

1977   Carter-Torrijos Treaty agreement to turn the Panama Canal over to Panama in 1999.

1978   Duncan's *Final de calle* wins Editorial Costa Rica prize and the Aquileo Echeverría National Prize for Literature the following year.

1980   Blas Jiménez's first of several books of poems to be published in the 1980s.

1982   First issue of the *Afro-Hispanic Review*, an important outlet for work by and about Black Hispanic writers.

1983   Norberto James moves to Boston.

1985   Jorge Artel awarded the National Prize for Poetry by the University of Antioquia.

1988   Zapata Olivella awarded the New Human Rights Prize for Literature granted by the National Assembly of France for *Lève toi mulâtre*.

1989   Estupiñán Bass awarded Ecuador's prestigious Condecoración Nacional al Mérito Cultural de Primera Clase.

Carlos Moore publishes his influential book *Castro, the Blacks and Africa* with its controversial speculation regarding Fidel Castro, Nicolás Guillén, and Nancy Morejón.

Death of Nicolás Guillén.

1990   Several books, both creative works and critical studies, in Afro-Hispanism published, a trend that continues unabated throughout the decade.

1993   Death of Nicomedes Santa Cruz.

1994   Death of Jorge Artel.

Chapter One

The Complexity of Complexion: Reading and Understanding Black Hispanic Writing

A black poet can only write from the Black experience. What else can they write from? They are Black. Whatever they write, whether it's exclusively about the beauty of flowers or the horrors of war or the deliciousness of a piece of chocolate cake, it's still an expression by a Black . . . and if they try to avoid putting any Blackness in there, it also says something. . . . The Black experience is any experience that a Black person has.

Gwendolyn Brooks

I speak to the black experience, but I am always talking about the human condition.

Maya Angelou

When Theodore O. Mason Jr. argued recently that a canon ought to be made up simply of texts worth reading,[1] he raised a problematic issue. Worth means different things to different people. For me, literature by Black Hispanic writers, which is often dogmatic and race specific, is worth reading in large measure because of what it reveals about the Black experience in Latin America. David William Foster recently challenged Hispanists to broaden our view beyond Borges and García Márquez to encompass the "vast riches" that such alternative voices as Black Hispanic writers offer.[2] J. Kubayanda also called for as much exposure to be given to the Black voice in Latin America as to the "voice of the masters."[3] Foster and Kubayanda are right; reading Black Hispanic literature forces readers to open their minds to multiple interpretations of or perspectives on reality.

If it is true, as we often hear, that people read books at least in part to discover things about themselves and their world, then Black Hispanic literature is a worthwhile place to start. Though race specific, Black writing represents authentic human experience. It also has the power to make people think because it is often laced with ambiguity, complexity, and controversy. This is due in large part to the practice of denial, a major obstacle that Blacks encounter in Latin America, where the presence of racism and even their very existence are frequently denied. It is thus no surprise that Blackness as identity is a major topic for the Black Hispanic writer, whether in class-conscious Cuba or in the Black-phobic Dominican Republic.

Black Hispanic writers address such topics as imperialism, oppression, slavery, racism, and race mixing, often within the framework of epic stories of Blacks on the move. We see this aggressive treatment of race in the works of Manuel Zapata Olivella and Cubena (Carlos Guillermo Wilson), in Adalberto Ortiz's novel of personal courage; in individual poems of Nicolás Guillén, Nancy Morejón, and Blas Jiménez; and uniquely in Norberto James's *Sobre la marcha*. These works are about heroism and courage, and their authors are themselves heroic in their determination not to be overlooked or deceived by the rhetoric of racial democracy. What they bring to the Hispanic canon are comprehensive explorations of the Black experience, in-depth insights into the Black psyche, and literary products that are at times challenging and even historically ambitious. Cubena's *Los nietos de Felicidad Dolores*, Guillén's *El diario que a diario*, and Zapata Olivella's *Changó, el gran putas*, for example, are works whose vision span's centuries. Black Hispanic writers do not always write about race, but when they do, their texts become privileged readings on this topic. Their struggle against racism and invisibility becomes especially evident when Blackness and nationalism— themes that are always intertwined in Black Hispanic literature but are not the same as Black nationalism—are portrayed.

Whether in the Hispanic Caribbean or in Central and South America, race is the fundamental issue in Afro-Hispanic literature. No amount of obfuscation[4] or arguments for regional identity, class consciousness, gender fairness, or "doing theory"[5] will alter this reality. For Black Hispanic authors, achieving literary Blackness is as important a goal as recognizing or acknowledging *mestizaje* (racial mixture) or what Nicolás Guillén once called "Cuban color." For this reason, the African heritage in Black Hispanic literature cannot be lost to a "cosmic-race-of-a-criticism" (Captain, 6) or to what I once called an "avant-garde criticism,"[6] in which complexity in the literary act is deemed, erroneously, to be more important than complexion.[7] Neither can we elevate the dialogue on racism to a higher plane that will somehow "go beyond it" (Captain, 6). As long as racism exists, how could one do so? When Cap-

tain states that the writer of African descent in Spanish America is part
of a Hispanic linguistic culture but also has a legitimate foothold in
another domain, she illustrates how being Black and Hispanic makes
this literature both the same as the wider literature but different from it
as well. She also underscores why achieving Black identity and expressing it in Spanish American literature is so complex.

Complexity in Afro-Hispanism cannot just refer to the act of writing
but must also address the racial question that motivates it. This does not
mean that Black Hispanic writers are not accomplished, daring, innovative, and even experimental, fully aware of aesthetic issues and the pro-
found questions of language in literature. Although some Black Hispanic writers have preferred instead to revel in the dignity of "popular"
verse or the "social" novel, recent "advanced" critical readings of the
works of Guillén,[8] Ortiz, Estupiñán Bass, and Nancy Morejón reveal a
deep interest in artistic innovation. Aida Cartagena Portalatín of the
Dominican Republic is another ground breaking writer though not discussed in this study.[9] It is thus a given that the intricacy and aesthetic
power of the literary work have to be taken into account, when dis-
cussing Black Hispanic writing, yet understanding the reality of race is
just as much our responsibility as readers and critics as appreciating the
language that expresses it. In this racial sense, *complexity* and *complexion*
in Latin America are interrelated terms. This is all the more true because
in addition to tackling racism and external denial, Black Hispanic writers have also had to address the complex obstacle of internal denial man-
ifested in the reluctance of some Black people themselves to identify
with Blackness.

This reluctance, which borders on the paranoia depicted in several
Black fictional characters (Antonio Angulo in Ortiz's *Juyungo,* Charles
McForbes in Quince Duncan's *Los cuatro espejos,* and José Antonio Pastrana in Nelson Estupiñán Bass's *El último río,* to name three of the most
prominent), is a by-product of the spectrum of racial color that exists in
Latin America. When Black people are attracted to the higher premium
at the lighter end of the spectrum, the mission of the Black writer who
wants to foster Black pride becomes problematic. This complexity represents what is most intriguing about Black Hispanic writers who are
themselves mulatto, or "half Black" in the Latin American sense. Such
writers, all of them Black in North American terms (where no distinction between Black and mulatto exists), include Guillén, who once
called himself "un mulato bastante bien claro" [a rather light-skinned
mulatto] but who also lamented living his "tragedia de ser negro"

[tragedy of being Black]; Ortiz, who agonized more than most over his own *mulatez* [mulatto status]; Estupiñán Bass, who acknowledged that race mixing was likely to be the way of the future;[10] Zapata Olivella, who confronted this issue in his autobiography *¡Levántate mulato!;* and even Manzano, the slave poet whose own father did not want him to play with *negritos* [little Black children]. While these writers raise the Black/mulatto distinction in their works, they confront it in their own identity as well.

Racial ambivalence and the issues it generates provide much of the tension that sustains such works as Ortiz's *Juyungo* and Zapata Olivella's *¡Levántate mulato!.* Controversies also contribute to that tension. The kind of controversies we find in Black Hispanic literature ranges from the radical themes of Zapata Olivella's *Chambacú* to Estupiñán Bass's extremism in *El último río.* We even find controversy in the ambiguous nature of Ortiz's message in *Juyungo.* The "lost" second part of Manzano's autobiography is still a hot topic of discussion. We do not even know what he left out of part one or why he wrote it in the first place. Guillén saw himself embroiled in controversy after controversy from the publication of his *Motivos de son* to the end of his career. For example, recent discussions of his work that focus on politics are encapsulated in the question, Did Guillén and Fidel Castro get along? This same question has also been applied to Nancy Morejón. The answer could well determine how we read some of their post-1959 poetry.[11]

What contributes to the authenticity of many of these texts (and to the controversies surrounding them) is that their authors are often as hard on those Blacks who do not take pride in Blackness as they are on Whites who practice racism. Positive Black role models abound in this literature, but Black Hispanic writers, leaving no obstacle to progress unchallenged, often take negative models to task. Readers will be enlightened by the balanced, honest, and often impassioned insights this literature brings to the Hispanic canon. We see this even-handed approach in *Motivos de son,* where Guillén offers an inside perspective by tackling divisive and disruptive racial practices in Cuba's Black community, and "Sabás," another early poem of his from the 1930s that finds more dignity for Blacks in hunger than in begging. We also find it in Cocambo, Ortiz's black antihero in *Juyungo.* We find it in the 1960s, in Estupiñán Bass's indictment in *El último río* of Blacks who exploit their own people, and in the 1990s, in the several negative Black characters in Cubena's *Los nietos de Felicidad Dolores,* in which some of the *nietos* [grandchildren] have not turned out as well as others. Black Hispanic writers do explore Black epic history, and they do write about heroic Black people on the move, but they are also aware of the multidimensional nature of the Black experience in Latin America.

The complexity of the Black experience in Latin America is particularly evident in such works as Quince Duncan's *Los cuatro espejos* that delve into the psyche of Black characters who represent the duality of a self uncertain of allegiance or place. Paranoia, behavioral traumas, and even the various kinds of *locura* [madness] we see in some of these works are related to racism. These extremes should not be unexpected from Blacks living, as one Black character ruminates, in a world that has produced a Hitler and apartheid and where Whiteness is prized and Blackness is not. Slavery and racism thus inform the vision of race displayed by these authors.

This vision, more than anything else, makes their key works worth reading, certainly to Black readers and critics. When Black critics read that the meaning and especially the significance of a work of art are conditioned by the intentions of the critic who reconstructs the work in the process of his or her reading (Mason, 15), we understand and agree fully because we come to this literature with a fixed purpose: to see what it tells us about Black people and the Black experience in Latin America and how effectively it does so. Different critics will, of course, have different hermeneutical strategies. A few years ago I tried to categorize these differences in Black Hispanic criticism into four main groups: Black criticism, characterized by a focus on race and ethnicity; negristic or socionegristic criticism, which focuses on folkloric, atavistic, and ethnological concerns; and Socialist, Marxist, or nationalist criticism and universal criticism, which examine the political implications of a work (the latter with a decidedly nonracial emphasis).[12] At the time I believed that by emphasizing revolutionary solidarity or *mestizaje,* Marxist, Socialist, and nationalist criticism aimed, like universal criticism, at "Whitening" the Black author by playing down his or her ethnic identity. Although these categories illustrate how the same works can be read and interpreted in different ways, I continue to believe that the Black criticism that goes beyond the literary in the first category helps us define and clarify what informs this literature and makes it worth reading.

The very discovery of a Black text makes it a readable item, and every critical reading, whether intentionally or not, is a celebration of the text's existence. Although the list of Hispanic canonical texts by Black authors is growing, it is not very long. Black critics thus understand that even if a Black work is subpar, it is still worth reading. Our intention is to find out as much about the subpar text as about the text that is a work of art because we know both can tell us something about Black life in the New World. If we can get this information from a Black poem, story, or novel, however crudely written, we still welcome it. The classic case in point is Manzano's slave autobiography. Over the years, the stylistic flaws of his *Autobiografía* have hardly diminished the importance of what is in it or of why he wrote it.

Any text by a Black Hispanic writer about Black people and the Black experience in Latin America is a privileged find, and for a time the main task in our field was simply to find them. The complexities of race and color in Latin America, however, sometimes make it difficult, as G.R. Coulthard recognized years ago,[13] to categorize works in this way. Janheinz Jahn tried to solve this problem by focusing his attention on the Black as theme rather than on the Black as author.[14] One of the first dialogues implicit in my earlier writings, as William Luis recognized, was between Jahn and me.[15] Both Jahn and I questioned the status of the author, myself in Black Hispanic literature in particular and Jahn in Neo-African literature, to use Jahn's term, in general. Jahn supports a criticism free from reference to or consideration of an author's color, whereas I do not. Luis was right to notice how I differ from Jahn. All of my work, including (and especially) my annotated bibliographies both in 1980 and in 1989, reflects this difference. In those works I tried to underscore my primary premise, which is that in Black Hispanic literature the identity of the author does matter, a view shared by Antonio Olliz Boyd, who a few years ago first developed his position on the subject in his doctoral dissertation.[16] The same applies to criticism written by Blacks about Black Hispanic writers; it should have this same basic premise built into its hermeneutical parameters. The question it raises is not one of biological determinism or mystical essentialism but of perspective.

Clearly not all Black people have the same perspective, and again, different critics have different intentions. Not all Black critics in Africa, the Caribbean, Latin America, or even in North America read the same way. One African critic, for example, whose own unique worldview and comparative knowledge of African writers and linguistics has enriched our discipline is the late J. Kubayanda of Ghana.[17] Kubayanda specialized in clarifying the African sources of Black Latin American literature by showing how principles of African versification are more appropriate tools for analysis than traditional European meter in such poems as

Guillén's "Negro bembón." He also challenged the acceptance of White, European, "universal" models that has been commonplace in Latin America since Columbus. His work is a constant repudiation of colonialism, neocolonialism, and any "ism" supporting the view that Western Whites have a monopoly on beauty, virtue, and intelligence. Kubayanda sought the African source of Blackness manifest in such principles as ancestrality, drum communication, ideophonic expression, plant symbolism, and heroic codes. Similarly, the Trinidadian Ian Smart emphasizes West Indianness because he is aware of the West Indian background of many of the Black writers in Central America.[18]

There are, of course, other critics who agree with Jahn's point of view. Alan Persico, for example, believes that it is unjustifiable to read the works of Black writers primarily as works of the Black experience;[19] we cannot consider a Black work to be a "new novel," for example, unless its Blackness is ignored or downplayed. In his pursuit of the stylistic and structural features of Black Hispanic literature, Persico would have us not focus on Black writers' "psychological and social enigmas, their crisis of identity, ethnic ambivalence and, in general, on their struggle for significance."[20] A Black perspective, however, cannot overlook these features, because when we take them out of our critical discussions, what is left? What is the point of reading Black Hispanic literature if we ignore the reasons that draw many Black readers to it in the first place? Persico later tries to focus on style and structure in Duncan's *Los cuatro espejos,* but his own discussion and conclusion show how hard it is to ignore content and theme in a Black Hispanic work even when the stated intent is to do so. Y. Captain-Hidalgo illustrates this difficulty in *The Culture of Fiction in the Works of Manuel Zapata Olivella* (Columbia: University of Missouri Press, 1993) by correctly arguing that the Afro-Colombian author's claim to universality lies precisely in his most specific emphasis on race.

My emphasis on race, Blackness, and racism also differs from Vera Kutzinski's approach. In her new book, Kutzinski takes issue with a number of tendencies in Afro-Hispanic literature and criticism, among them the "masculine poetics" of the *negrista* (yet largely white) poets of the 1930s in the Hispanic Caribbean.[21] Such poets, in her view, turn the non-White woman's body into a sexual object. She also takes exception to "image" studies. Kutzinski nevertheless focuses a great deal of attention on the problematic "representation" of women in *negrista* poetry, condemning what she perceives as degrading images and racial stereotypes, one of which is the *mulata* [the "half" Black, "half" White female]. She also laments the absence ("erasure") of White women in Afro-Cuban and Cuban historical poetry, including some works by Nicolás Guillén. One of the problems with her study, however, is her intimation that in Afro-Hispanic studies indiscriminate charges of racism are brought, presumably by Blacks, against all Whites who write about African-American cultures, but this is true only for those guilty of it. To paraphrase Malcolm X, Blacks do not hate all Whites, only those who practice racism. Another problem with her study, which looks at *poesía negra/mulata* [Black/mulatto poetry] as a gender issue, is that in defending the Black, the *mulata*, and the non-Black woman represented in Caribbean writing, Kutzinski lumps Black and non-Black writers together, and this does not work because they do stand apart. For example, despite the "homosocial" structures she finds in a number of Guillén's early Afro-Cuban poems, Guillén himself dismisses *negrista* poetry as "circumstantial tourism" (Kutzinski, 13). He also characterizes Luis Pales Matos's treatment of Blacks as "superficial."[22]

In her reading of Black Hispanic literature, Kutzinski also misses the point entirely regarding Quince Duncan. Apparently not being familiar with this Black Costa Rican writer, she uses his *Final de calle* [*Street's End*] as an example of a non-Black novel by a Black writer to support her contention that Blacks do not always write about Blacks. She does not understand that Duncan wrote this "White" and therefore more "Costa Rican" book anonymously and without Black content consciously as a test to destroy the myth that his Black heritage gave him some advantage in the world of Costa Rican letters.[23] The novel won a National Prize for Literature, though Duncan believes that his "Black" books, which have never won, are better. Kutzinski focuses on masculine biases, but her book primarily concerns Hispanic Caribbean literature about White male sexuality and non-White women.

Lourdes Martínez-Echazábal's recent work also goes to the heart of the controversial issue of race not in the Caribbean, which is Kutzinski's domain, but in South American literature.[24] She discusses novels in which the key race relationships are between White women and non-White men, focusing particularly on the Blackness factor and its impact on authors in Latin America's racially mixed societies. My own position differs from hers; she downplays Black identity, while I not only highlight it but also see the issue of race in Latin America as being not much different in North America. The issue is the same in both places, as I believe Martínez-Echazábal will learn as she reads more of the literature of Black Hispanic authors themselves, especially those writing today.

This is not to say, however, that these writers have not grappled with the problem that race mixing presents. Martínez-Echazabal's emphasis on this theme in what she calls "Mulatto fiction" is valid because it does exist, but again in Black Hispanic literature it clearly makes a difference who is doing the writing. And because few of the authors whom Martínez-Echazábal discusses are Black or even mulatto, the authenticity of her examples is questionable. Rather, we should highlight and examine literary Blackness in texts written by Black Hispanic writers themselves.

Just as the Latin American version of flight from Blackness occurs in the United States, the North American Black/White polarization occurs in Latin America as well. Both result from racist pressures and I, as a Black critic, am especially interested in charting how the Black Hispanic writer deals with and expresses these pressures in literature. Black Hispanic writers create out of ethnic memory. I read this literature, certainly the representative works I discuss in the following chapters, in the same way.[25]

Chapter Two

Biography and Black Autobiography: Black Hispanic Writers and the Autobiographical Statement

All literature, everything that one writes, is, in a way, an autobiographical statement.

Adalberto Ortiz

My primary purpose in this chapter is to focus on what Black Hispanic authors themselves have written about their outlooks, their work, and their lives, and thus the above quotation from Ortiz serves as a perfect opener. Every writer, he believes, makes a confession that relates to the writer's thought and experience. This self-revelation is one of the strongest factors tempting such Black critics as myself to read Black Hispanic literature.

Black autobiography is not a primary genre in Latin America, but a few examples do exist. Among the early books, Juan Francisco Manzano's *Autobiografía* (1835) comes to mind, as do Candelario Obeso's *Lectura para ti* [*For You*, 1878] and *Lucha de la vida* [*Life struggle*, 1882] and more recently Nicolás Guillén's *Páginas vueltas* [*Turned Pages*, 1982] and Manuel Zapata Olivella's *¡Levántate mulato!* [*Mulatto, Arise!*, 1987]. Autobiographical writings, however, come in different forms, and in this sense Black Hispanic writers over the years have made numerous statements in the first person singular.

Biographies of Black Hispanic writers are also in short supply but by no means nonexistent. Probably the first of these was Francisco Calcagno's *Poetas de color* [*Poets of Color*], which detailed the lives and work of the nineteenth-century Cuban poets Gabriel de la Concepción Valdés (Plácido) and Juan Francisco Manzano; a portion of it was first published in 1868 in a newspaper.[1] As we shall see in the next chapter, the slave poet's life is a favorite topic among researchers in Afro-Hispanism. Roberto Friol's more recent work on Manzano is particularly invaluable.[2]

In his biographical study of Candelario Obeso, Vicente Caraballo traces the life of "the Colombian Othello," as he was known, from infancy and touches on controversial topics including the poet's untimely death, at the age of 35.[3] Laurence Prescott also took up the story of Obeso, focusing on the poet's works and his frustration at living in a racist society.[4] Concha Peña wrote a biographical study of the Afro-Panamanian Gaspar Octavio Hernández, the Modernist poet known as the Black Swan, who was troubled by similar frustrations.[5] Ivan Augusto Gómez argued that Octavio Hernández's life is expressed in his poetry and that no other biographical information is necessary.[6] He could have a point if we use his "Ergo sum" as an example.[7] This poem is similar to Manzano's "Mis treinta años" ["My thirty Years"].[8] Both are sonnets, and each gives a profile of the poet's psychological state as well as physical features in Octavio Hernández's case. In one poem we have the pain of bondage, and in the other the pain of being opposite to Whiteness. Although we feel Manzano's pain in his "Mis treinta años," the *Autobiografía,* as Sylvia Molloy has argued,[9] is the best self-portrait we have of him.

Leopoldo Horrego Estuch reviews Martín Morúa Delgado's life and works[10] as does Morúa Delgado's Afro-Cuban compatriot Nicolás Guillén,[11] who also had something to say about his Afro-Colombian colleagues: Obeso, his precursor, and Jorge Artel, his contemporary. Guillén observes from the outset that Morúa Delgado, who was both a writer and a political figure, was the first and last Black Cuban to reach the high post of president of the Senate. Angel Augier's 1947 work is the standard biography of Guillén himself,[12] although several other books, some of which are mentioned in the next chapter, have appeared since. Adalberto Ortiz found a biographer in Ronna Newman, although her work, which was enriched by her personal correspondence with the author, has never been published to my knowledge.[13]

Pilar Barrios wrote his own biographical statement.[14] Born in 1889, Barrios focuses on an incident that stands out in his childhood: being taken out of school by those entrusted with his education with the justification that because he was black, he was not going to go far academically. The stigma of inferiority was set early and, as I discuss in a later chapter, he spent his long life—he died in 1979—urging equality in intelligence for himself and other Blacks. The keys to success, he stressed to Black youth, were study and preparation. Barrios also tells us that at the age of 19 he dedicated some *décimas* entitled "Mi madre" to his mother. In later life Barrios became known, in part, for his poems in respect of Black mothers and women.

Several biographers have taken an interest in Manuel Zapata Olivella, Y. Captain-Hidalgo most recently,[15] but beyond that not many biographies of other Black Hispanic writers have been undertaken. Ironically three of the four Black Hispanic authors most written about (Manzano, Guillén, and Zapata Olivella) are three who also have written autobiographies. Biographies and biographical sketches—even some fictionalized ones—abound on Plácido, the fourth most written about, including Frederick Stimson's work, which is the only book in English on this poet.[16] Plácido's biographers explore all aspects, certainly the controversial ones, of his life, work, and death. And like all of the writers discussed here, he left us such autobiographical works as the poems "La plegaria a Díos," "Adios a mi lira," and "Despedida a mi madre," all of which were written in the final days of his life.[17]

In addition to literature, many Black Hispanic writers have given interviews that were published or recorded in which they reveal how they view society, their work, and themselves and cover important aspects of their lives, identifying for the reader/listener salient features or defining moments or incidents in their lives, often associated with Blackness and color awareness, that have shaped their literary outlook and direction. This has been a welcome development, especially over the past few years. Sometimes what they say in these interviews as well as in letters, memoirs, articles, and critical writings captures the essence of what they are about better than the information conveyed in biographical details. Sometimes the interview is an invitation to peer inside their *intrahistoria,* or inner history, where motivation and anything else that makes them tick as an author lie hidden. Fortunately there is a tremendous amount of documentary material of this kind to draw on. We see this to good measure in Cubena's recent interview with Elba Birmingham-Pokorny,[18] especially where he talks of the impact of his *chombo* experience in Panama and of his life as a Black of Hispanic origin in the United States. Cubena also talks of the mission that defines all his work: to present a positive image of Blacks, which he has done repeatedly in his poetry, stories, and novels. I discuss Cubena's recent work, which is autobiographical, in chapter 7, but this interview as well as others he has given add to our knowledge.

Another good example of first-person insight is Norberto James's informative introduction of himself that he provides in the article "First Person Singular?",[19] which I return to in chapter 8. Among its revelations is that he does not write consciously as a poet of negritude. He also acknowledges that seeing the racial problem in the United States firsthand helped him understand the problem of race in the Dominican Republic.

The United States figures prominently in the autobiographical statements of many Black Hispanic authors. As if to sum up his lifelong antipathy toward the United States, Nicolás Guillén told Laurence Prescott in one of his last interviews that the worst thing American Blacks have is American Whites although he acknowledged, at the same time, that there are many Whites who are friends of Blacks.[20] Guillén, like Norberto James and many other black Hispanic writers, had visited the United States, first in 1937 and again in 1952, and his experiences both times solidified his disgust with the country. Writing about sojourns north in his memoirs, Guillén says that seeing Harlem and the separation imposed on that black community left him, even years later, with a feeling of anguish not easily forgotten despite the long time that had passed since being there.[21]

Guillén published *Páginas vueltas* in 1982. One is left with three overriding impressions from reading these memoirs. First, throughout his early years Guillén was surrounded by Blacks as well as Whites, from his White uncle to his Black *abuela* [grandmother], and his racial consciousness was acute. Second, his father was a strong formative force in his early life and remained so throughout his life. Third, the "Yankee" presence was a factor early in his life and thereafter in his consciousness. Although harsh at times, Guillén does show tact and discretion in his memoir with regard to the United States. He is careful, for example, to term his lifelong opposition to its policies as *rebeldía* [rebellion] and not *odio* [hate]. What I find especially informative in *Páginas vueltas* is learning from Guillén himself what he considered to be his three most significant books: *Motivos de son* (1930), *West Indies Ltd.* (1934), and *Elegía a Jesús Menéndez* [Elegy to Jesús Menéndez, 1948–1951]. In all three the "Yankee presence" is decidedly strong, and each book, Guillén thought, represented a significant milestone in his development. Guillén has often talked about the reception of *Motivos de son* and the controversy its publication generated from its publication in the 1930s and through the present. In his later conversation with Prescott, Guillén confessed that these poems dazzled with rhythms and made people laugh but that underneath it all was a social intent and that a couple of them at least made people think.

One of Guillén's most poignant statements about his early life is contained in another interview, this one from 1976 with Orlando Castellanos. First published in 1989 a few months after Guillén's death, this is one of the last interviews he gave.[22] Read in tandem with the first pages of *Páginas vueltas,* it provides fine insight into the young Guillén growing up in a racially polarized society in a family "of color," a term used at the time to avoid the shame of being called "Black." The discrimination, racism, and scorn heaped on non-Whites in those days not too far removed from the era of slavery and the humiliations they had to endure remained etched in his memory. Guillén would say that he was not Black "like Kid Chocolate," but even as a mulatto he suffered the barbs of prejudice.

Guillén gave numerous interviews adding to and corroborating his memoirs. Under the heading "Conversación con Nicolás Guillén," Nancy Morejón put together a collage of interviews with Guillén, including one conducted specifically for the occasion.[23] Here Guillén outlined several of the earlier defining moments in his life: his father's death, the fall of Machado, joining the Communist Party, and the Spanish Civil War. Guillén also makes his now famous assertion that he was not a poet of negritude. He made the same claim to Keith Ellis in another interview.[24] He also told Ellis that he did not believe Langston Hughes had influenced his work. The two poets had a long friendship that started back in the 1930s when Guillén had the task of interviewing this already famous Black American on a visit to Cuba. In recently published letters from Hughes written in the 1930s, the "seasoned" veteran advised the then "novice" Guillén how to handle the fame his *Motivos de son* would bring him.[25]

Manuel Zapata Olivella's meeting with Langston Hughes took place in New York in the 1940s, and he describes it in *He visto la noche [I Have Seen the Night,* 1974], which he wrote in 1946 and first published in 1953.[26] This little book is full of information about his experiences in the United States, some of which he revisits in later interviews; it bears witness to the growing racial consciousness of that time. In a recent conversation with Yvonne Captain-Hidalgo, for example, Zapata Olivella said that he identifies with the United States through Langston Hughes; when he thinks of that country, he sees it through Langston Hughes's eyes, even now after his death.[27] On his journey to the United States in the 1940s, Zapata Olivella carried in his backpack a copy of Hughes's book *The Big Sea.* Meeting Langston Hughes was a significant event in the lives of both Guillén and Zapata Olivella. This acquaintance fed into their sense of racial identity. In a series of recent publications, most notably in *¡Levántate mulato!,* which expands on the topics discussed in *He visto la noche* and is discussed in chapter 5, Zapata Olivella makes it

known what he considers most important in human life—our understanding of "who we are."

Both Nicolás Guillén and Zapata Olivella have written memoirs, but
each laid the groundwork for these larger works over the years through
shorter works or through responses to scholarly and personal inquiry.
Páginas vueltas, ¡Levántate mulato!, and their other autobiographical
statements are instructive for the insights the authors provide on forces
and events that shaped them and their literature. Key among these are
the negative personal experiences suffered in their youth because of their
color and the enormous influence their fathers had on their lives.

The racist perception of Blackness that plagued their nineteenth-
century predecessors continue to be a concern for Black writers in the
twentieth century. Color and race have always been in the forefront of
Adalberto Ortiz's thoughts. In a conversation with Ronna Newman, his
biographer, Ortiz discusses his novel *Juyungo,* which, he tells us, did not
require a great deal of research because he grew up in the area and was
familiar with the characters that he depicted.[28] In an interview with
Michael Walker in 1976, Ortiz tells how he set out in that novel to mine
the virgin, uncharted waters of the black experience in Ecuador.[29] Newman agrees that Ortiz's literary creations reveal much about his background, sentiments, and attitudes, including the political solution in the
novel, which was influenced by his leftist views at the time. On other
occasions Ortiz would recall the Black province of Esmeraldas where he
grew up and that was to shape his literature and his mixed opinions in
later years regarding his own racial identity and the question of racial
duality. Stanley Cyrus was one of the first critics to show how comments
that Ortiz makes on ethnic ambivalence in *Juyungo* are similar to statements that he made about himself many years later because of his being
a mixture of Black and White.[30] His literature does indeed show him
grappling with this dilemma; when he talks about his own literary personality not being very well defined or uniform, we know he is referring
to it. Despite all this, however, Ortiz did not debase Blacks and is in fact
partial to them. In his poetry Ortiz tells us, as do some of his fictional
characters, that he would rather be Black than White. In a conversation
with Antonio Planells, Ortiz reiterates his belief that all literature is
autobiographical, certainly his own.[31]

Both Ortiz and his compatriot Nelson Estupiñán Bass write in other
genres but express pride in their mastery of the novel. Ortiz tells us he
was a poet and short story writer before becoming a novelist; *Juyungo,*
his first novel, grew out of a short story and in his view can be consid-

ered a long poem in prose form, heavily imbued as it is with the rhythms and music of the Black poetry he was writing at the time. Nelson Estupiñán Bass confesses in an interview with Henry Richards that while he writes poetry and plays, he considers the novel to be the best medium for expressing his vision of the world.[32] Estupiñán Bass remembers that he wrote and published his first poem, "Canto a la Quinceañera," in 1934. Other poetry followed, but he is known primarily as a prolific novelist whose novel *El último río,* as we will see in chapter 4, is a trenchant exploration of the Black psyche. It is important that Blacks write about Blacks, he tells Millicent Bolden,[33] because one must emphasize and not deny identity, even if that denial would lead to economic parity. There is no reason for Black people to be ashamed of their color, a message he tries to get across in all of his works. Estupiñán Bass underscores this point by arguing that Blacks should be proud to call themselves Black rather than Brown [*moreno*], the term some Esmeraldan Blacks now seem to prefer. Estupiñán Bass tells her, however, that love has no boundaries, and he is ready to admit that if José Vasconcelos's "Cosmic Race" comes to pass, so be it.

Identity is a recurring theme in many of these autobiographical statements. Cristina Rodríguez Cabral and Luz Argentina Chiriboga have both addressed the fundamental issue of writing as it relates to identity. Chiriboga attacks stigma and racial shame in her novel *Bajo la piel de los tambores* [*Under the Drumskins,* 1991], and she is especially sensitive to the many ways racial insults are perpetrated against (and internalized by) Blacks. Recently Chiriboga used the interview format to reinforce her views on race in Ecuador where, she says (agreeing with Nelson Estupiñán Bass), people do not want to recognize their Black identity, even in Esmeraldas where there is a large Black population.[34] Rodríguez Cabral, who writes prose and poetry, does the same in Uruguay. In her interview with Lorna Williams, this new writer talks about the need to raise Black esteem and preserve Black culture in her country.[35] She also questions whether her own poetry can be considered Black because until recently she had made no special effort to imbue it with "Black" language.

Jorge Artel used an interview to talk of his life and voluntary exile from Colombia for 23 years following three months as a political prisoner. In his conversations with Laurence Prescott who would in later years write a book about him, Artel tells of many "long forgotten racial and political incidents which had challenged his dignity yet bolstered his sense of identity."[36] Antonio Acosta Márquez also talked of the pain of exile from Venezuela in the introduction to his book of poems.[37] In his interview with Elena Poniatowska, Nicomedes Santa Cruz takes a stand against cultural domination, or the elitist view in Peru that popular poetry is inferior.[38] This defense goes to the heart of what the poet is about because as we will see in chapter 9, Santa Cruz writes popular poetry, which he thinks should not take a back seat to or even be differentiated from so-called erudite poetry. Santa Cruz, *decimista,* also wrote Black poetry in other forms and does not think that poetry should take a back seat either. In the introduction to one of his collections of poetry, Santa Cruz indicated how his new poems on Blacks and Black themes caused quite a stir when they first came out. He does not call them Black poems, more than likely objecting to the way some would use that label—like popular poetry—to dismiss them, but he speaks proudly of the new direction his poetry has taken.[39]

Nicomedes Santa Cruz objected to labels, as did Nicolás Guillén many times, and so did Nancy Morejón. Her "Mujer negra," according to the poet herself, was not written as a banner for Blacks or for women. In her interview with Rafael Rodríguez, the Afro-Cuban poet explained how she personally saw something symbolic, universal, and unlimited in the title, which is her way of rejecting labels.[40] Morejón's compatriot, Pedro Pérez Sarduy, uses his recent interview with Magdalena García-Pinto to update readers on details of his early life, works, and current whereabouts,[41] but he also uses an open letter to Carlos Moore to put Cuba and the racial experience in perspective. Politics and ideology continue to complicate the search for Black identity in Cuba, and even though outsiders looking in might be confused, Black Cubans, Pérez Sarduy writes, "know full well who we are."[42]

Critical writings by Black Hispanic writers offer a wealth of autobiographical statements. Adalberto Ortiz's treatise on negritude in Latin America, which has been translated into English and published in an easily available and prestigious collection of critical essays, is a good example.[43] Nelson Estupiñán Bass, Manuel Zapata Olivella, Nicomedes Santa Cruz, and others have all provided readers with critical insights not just on their own literature but on that of others as well.[44] Much of this critical writing addresses negritude, slavery, and the Black image in literature and questions whether White writers can create credible and authentic images of non-White people, and much of it confirms that the Black critical perspective in Latin America is not too different from that found in racially polarized North America. Hispanic Black writers believe that their personal experience enables them to most accurately portray the Black experience, and they tell us so. Martín Morúa Delgado questioned Villaverde's antislavery novel in the late nineteenth century and set about writing a better one of his own. Juan Pablo Sojo in the early twentieth century attacked Rómulo Gallegos's depiction of Blacks in Barlovento, eventually writing his own novel on the same subject. Quince Duncan lambasted Whites who write about Black life from a distance. And Nicolás Guillén roundly rejected the superficiality of poetic *negrismo* and the damaging image of Blacks that White *negrista* poets from the 1920s, 1930s, and beyond have left, singling out the "Black" poetry of Luis Palés Matos for criticism.

Black Hispanic writers assess the work of others, but they talk about their own work as well. Adalberto Ortiz, Quince Duncan, Antonio Preciado, and Nancy Morejón, among others, have all offered self-assessments. Morejón has made as many substantive comments about her "Mujer negra" as anyone else. The same can be said of Guillén and his *son* poems. Norberto James guides the reader to his social and political poetry. In several of his interviews, Manuel Zapata Olivella has talked extensively about his novel *Changó, el gran putas.* Gregorio Martínez tells us, in an interview with Luis Freire, that Candelario, his black protagonist in *Canto de sirena* [*The Siren's Song, 1977*]—likely an autobiographical work—is the collective conscience and spokesperson for marginalized, exploited people in his native Peru.[45] Duncan, in his interview with Ian Smart, explains that his protagonist in *Los cuatro espejos,* who had to learn to accept himself, clearly is not Duncan because the author knows who he is; he does tell Smart, however, that the short story "Una canción en la magrugada ["A Song at Dawn", 1970]," which is about a young Black boy taken away from his coastal community where Caribbean English is spoken to live in an all Spanish-speaking community, is heavily autobiographical. Duncan adds that the strongest literary influence on him came from North American writers, James Baldwin and William Faulkner in particular.

Finally, one of the most remarkable autobiographical statements of all is Carlos Arturo Truque's "Mi testimonio" ("My Testimony," no date) whose protagonist is "a normal man" who speaks of his life as lacking in importance aside from the suffering that fate has dealt him.[46] In reviewing his life, Truque tells how he was a good student born into a town of Blacks in Colombia and of learning in his eighth year, when he moved from his hometown to Cali, that being Black made a difference. Manuel Zapata Olivella had the same revelation when he went away to university in Bogotá. In Cali, Truque was denied a pass in his third year of school despite having done well. Truque tells us he was never able to rid himself of the memory of that injustice or of the man responsible for it. Both came to symbolize his life-long exposure to the grievous wrongs against him, his writings, and others like him. Truque, who died in 1970, writes as a victim who yet "held firm" in the hope that those who came after would have "a purer life, one that we did not have the opportunity to live" (Truque, 22).

Chapter Three

Slavery and the Pivotal Afro-Cubans: Juan Francisco Manzano's *Autobiografía*, Nicolás Guillén's *El diario que a diario*, and Nancy Morejón's "Mujer negra"

> Blacks in Cuba, as in other Latin American countries, live with the psychological legacy of centuries of white domination.
>
> Ingrid Peritz

Of all the candidates to be considered for inclusion in the Hispanic canon, one can easily begin with the pivotal Afro-Cubans: Juan Francisco Manzano, Nicolás Guillén, and Nancy Morejón. Each one, in his or her own time, has been a standard-bearer in Afro-Hispanism, and as a group they are among the first names to come to mind when representative Black Hispanic writers are discussed. Guillén, of course, is the first among equals and, in effect, has already been canonized. Manzano and Morejón are close behind. Critical interest in all three of these Afro-Cuban writers has recently intensified for different reasons,[1] but what interests me here is the link to slavery. Manzano is Latin America's most celebrated slave poet; Morejón is the author of "Mujer negra," which has been called as fine a treatment of slavery by any of her generation;[2] and Nicolás Guillén, like Nancy Morejón, is known for many things, among them his own poems on Black slavery.[3]

It is no surprise that the Afro-Cubans are pivotal on both canon inclusion and the subject of slavery. That infamous institution had the longest run in Cuba of all the Hispanic countries, and it has had an equally enduring presence as a theme in Cuban literature. Much of this literary focus on slavery and its legacy dates back to Manzano and his influential *Autobiografía* (1835), the only extant narrative written in Spanish by a slave, which alone should guarantee it a place in the Hispanic canon. Morejón's "Mujer negra" has done more than any other single poem to focus attention not only on the Black female slave in Cuban history but also on contemporary Afro-Cuban women like the one who wrote it. Guillén himself focused some of this attention on her in "Nancy," a prose poem he wrote in praise of her and her "dark skin" and "African head."[4] Guillén admired Morejón for her poetry, which he characterized as "black like her skin," but he also recognized that her work is at the same time "deeply Cuban."

Manzano made his mark as author of what has become a nineteenth-century prototext and as a living prototype for abolitionism and anti-slavery literature. [Guillén and Afro-Cubanism are often taken as synonymous terms,] and Morejón and her work inevitably arise in any discussion of feminism, Afro-Hispanism, and the Black woman writer today. What makes these Afro-Cuban authors special, in part, is that all three have been risk takers: Manzano risked his life to write and wrote about slavery, both uncommon adventures for a slave; [Guillén first took risks with his *Motivos de son* (1930), a small collection of poems that incorporated Black life, talk, and rhythms into Cuban literature back when such heroic acts were rare;[5]] and Morejón dared to write about the use and the abuse of the Black female slave at a time in Cuba when highlighting race was considered divisive.

The search for Black identity in Hispanic literature began with Juan Francisco Manzano, and it is appropriate to begin this discussion with him. His legacy lives on in the writing of his Afro-Cuban compatriots and other twentieth-century Black Hispanic writers who have not forgotten the past. His main desires were for his own personal freedom and for the freedom to write, both not unrelated to the search for respect that Black Hispanic writers seek today, a respect that canon representation will help confer.

Manzano is an admirable example of heroism because writing about his life was just as dangerous as living it. Like his contemporary Plácido (Gabriel de la Concepción Valdés), he had to be careful about what he put down on paper. Plácido, a free nineteenth-century revolutionary Black poet, was accused of being the leader of a conspiracy, *la Conspiración de la Escalera* [the Ladder Conspiracy], to free the slaves. His diatribes against slavery and tyranny were subtle, often hidden in fables and doubletalk, but not subtle enough because his poems helped to condemn him to death by firing squad. Manzano, for his part, learned to write, which was unusual for slaves—in fact, they were forbidden to do so. Writing became one of the obsessions of his life. The autobiography

he left us, even with its contradictions, is a remarkable account of a sur-
vivor of slavery who willed himself the knowledge to be able to write
about it, which was in itself a heroic act. He was dependent on the pru-
dence of white sponsors for protection but took the chance in the hope
that telling his story would help him attain the freedom he so desper-
ately desired.

Manzano's poems, as he himself readily admitted, were simply imita-
tions of models he had handy, but his autobiography was to be something
else. He initially planned to include everything—certainly the most interesting parts—but backpedaled a bit after consideration when he realized
that to do so might be too risky (and would require reams of paper). He
decided a few months later to keep the most interesting parts to himself,
reserving them for a later work, a "truly Cuban" novel he hoped to write
once freed and secure. Manzano, as Jill Netchinsky recently wrote, was
nobody's fool.[6] In her view Manzano really fancied himself a budding
author who wanted to use his self-taught talent for gain in the same way
that Whites did. Just as he had used poetry readings to his advantage, he
also hedged on his exposé, thus driving up the market value of his future
revelations presumably about the horrors of slavery.

Although he did describe some incidents of suffering, Manzano was
the first to admit that he had skipped over some of the horrors of slavery. The care that he took in being circumspect as to what to include
and what to leave out of his work has given rise to several questions that
critics and literary historians have subsequently had to address. For
example, Lorna Williams's new book, the most recent in English on the
representation of slavery in Cuban fiction, addresses the issue of authenticity in the slave protagonists' testimony, including Manzano's *Autobiografía,* in a chapter subtitled "Narrating the Unspeakable" (Williams,
21–51). Achieving narrative candor was a definite challenge for Manzano because he was writing his exposé of slavery while the slave owner
who tormented him the most was still alive. In another recent book in
English on slavery in the Cuban narrative, William Luis correctly states
that Manzano's life is a testament of the cruelties of the slavery system
(Luis, 85) and emphasizes how he describes the violation of slavery laws
by his owner and nemesis the Marquesa de Prado Ameno. Manzano
exposes the evils of slavery, Luis argues, to persuade the reader into
assuming an antislavery position. However, he goes on to state that
Manzano's descriptions of such evils are offset by other scenes that con-
tradict his own indictment of slavery; this ambivalence is taken as evidence of Manzano's strong desire to document the happier moments

under that same oppressive system. Luis concludes that Manzano's auto-biography is an honest and complete picture of both bad and good masters. Luis misses the point here because what Manzano was doing, I believe, was giving his benefactor and friend Domingo Del Monte what he wanted: an account of slavery that showed how it could be improved or reformed, namely, by policing the bad masters more closely. Williams also disagrees with Luis by questioning whether Manzano's depiction of both the good and the bad moments under slavery really confirms his honesty.

According to Luis, the trauma that Manzano experiences is a result of his going back and forth between good and evil masters, although the real trauma occurred when he sat down to write the unspeakable; he had to describe his experiences as a slave in a way that would not bring reprisal. Manzano agreed to go ahead with his story only after receiving assurances from his benefactor that he would be protected. Luis correctly sees this fear of reprisal as a factor in Manzano's writing and, more importantly, believes this fear may also explain what Luis calls the text's "silent" moments in reference to the poet's decision not to tell the reader about the horrors of slavery, limiting himself instead to what he calls the "essential accounts."

These silent moments bring us back to the "unspeakable" in Williams's subtitle. Manzano had to suppress significant events in his narrative, and that is no way to speak honestly or get to the authentic self. Whether or not he was instructed by Del Monte to omit "the worst part" from his narrative, as Williams conjectures, or encouraged by Del Monte to stress the "unhappy moments" under slavery, as Luis suggests, we do not know, but we do know that Manzano did modify and edit his personal experiences in the *Autobiografía*. Unlike Luis, who argues that Manzano's autobiography gives us a complete and honest picture, Williams wonders whether there were ever any good moments under slavery. Pointing to Manzano's bad memory, inconsistencies, and discrepancies as well as gaps in the narrative, radical shifts in perception, and doubts the narrator himself casts on the veracity of his own words, Williams concludes quite reasonably that Manzano's early childhood was not as carefree as he claims it was and that even the good mistress, Doña Beatriz, may not have pampered him to the extent reported in the early pages of the text.[7]

In any event, Manzano's *Autobiografía* is a fascinating text that readers should value both for what he put in and for what he left out. His story, the best effort of a self-taught slave, is the first of many Black His-

panic stories that help document the New World authentically; even
with its troubling contradictions, it is remarkable. Manzano has been
critically "resurrected" in recent years,[8] and his reputation has undergone a metamorphosis; he's no longer the young *negro bueno* [good
Negro] or *mansocordero* [meek sheep] I myself once considered him to be[9]
but rather an adult writer looking back and trying to set down his life
story in an acceptable way.

Vera Kutzinski is right to say that we can no longer castigate such
nineteenth-century non-White writers as Plácido and Manzano for their
presumed lack of racial awareness (Kutzinski 1993, 12). Their writings
do address the complexities of their own racial situations. Manzano,
along with Plácido, was a legend in his time, and his literary and historical worth justifies a valued place for him in the Hispanic canon in our
time. In fact, one of the insights of Mercedes Rivas's recent work is her
contention that what separates Manzano in his *Autobiografía* from such
fictional protagonists as Sab and Francisco, two of the better-known fig-
ments of White nineteenth-century antislavery imagination, is that
Manzano ran away to escape a slavery he could no longer tolerate (Rivas,
231). This run to freedom in Havana that serves as the climax of his
autobiography, together with the day-to-day details he gives of his life,
sets his work apart and makes his story worth reading today.

Although he was aware that his story was to be used for abolitionist
purposes, especially abroad, Manzano was not the public voice that Plácido was, and neither did he want to be. Manzano did not strive to be a
voice for Blacks; he was his own voice. After a life in slavery, he simply
wanted to be left alone, perhaps to write, and he hoped his autobiography would earn him that solitude and that privilege, especially because
he had taken a wife.[10] His hopes were high, but after gaining his freedom, he found that a free Black voice was considered more dangerous
than an enslaved one. Manzano was practically forced into silence following the Ladder Conspiracy and the subsequent purge that doomed
Plácido, who denounced him during the aftermath of that failed effort,
perhaps thinking the ex-slave poet too private and uninvolved with the
cause of Black freedom or too closely associated with Del Monte, whom
Plácido also denounced.[11] Plácido may have realized that Del Monte,
despite helping (and using) Manzano, thought very little not only of the
activist Plácido in particular but of Blacks in general, considering them
"one of the most backward races in the human family."[12]

Manzano must have been tremendously disillusioned when freedom
did not bring him the peace and security he had so desired. Rather, he

was jailed and tortured before finally convincing the authorities of his innocence, something that Plácido was unable to do. Manzano was effectively silenced, with the exception of a few poems, after the purge, which is unfortunate because he was the only significant, well-known Black voice left after Plácido's death. He certainly did not write the great Cuban novel he at one time had expressed interest in writing. Yet, though silenced in his time, Manzano's voice, like Plácido's, is still heard today. These two poets, who were somewhat of rivals in their day, really are two sides of the same coin. Manzano wanted the personal liberty that should be everyone's right, and Plácido worked hard to achieve that right for others. History has been kinder to Manzano, I believe, than to Plácido; the former has been lauded for his attempts at literature and pitied for the abuse he suffered as a slave, whereas the latter has been criticized for wasting his talent on occasional verse, and his role as hero is not widely accepted. However, Plácido already had what Manzano wrote to achieve—freedom—but literally gave it up, along with his life, for a cause. In short, Plácido was clearly a public voice who used his poetry as a platform to further causes. Manzano was a private poet who tried to use public fame to ensure a private existence. Neither Plácido nor Manzano escaped notice of the authorities. Both paid dearly for daring to write.

Several years ago, J. Kubayanda anticipated Kutzinski's views on the racial awareness of these two poets when he noticed in Plácido's combativeness a foreshadowing of the Black Renaissance of the 1920s, the Afro-Cuban Movement of the 1930s, and the Civil Rights Movement of the 1960s.[13] Kubayanda believed as well that the writings of both Manzano and Plácido reflect a pioneering attempt to create a literature of resistance, freedom, and justice, precisely the same concerns that modern Black writers have taken up in their literature.

What also makes Manzano remarkable is that his *Autobiografía* generated or provided a model for several subsequent antislavery works of fiction by White Cuban intellectuals. Anselmo Suárez y Romero, for example, edited Manzano's autobiography, altering its original spelling, grammar, and syntax; under its inspiration he then wrote *Francisco,* a novel that circulated in manuscript form among the Del Monte circle. There it came to the attention of Antonio Zambrana, who years later penned a version of his own, which he called *El negro Francisco.* William Luis writes that "with some variation . . . Manzano's life and writings would be repeated by other antislavery writers. . . . [his] autobiography determined the direction in which the antislavery narrative would unfold" (Luis, 39). Many White authors were, indeed, in "literary bondage" to Manzano. From Manzano, however, we get the real thing. He leads off this grouping of Black canonical candidates because, however tempered, whatever version we read—and there are several that have been worked over by different "white hands"[14]—we know that Manzano's own words, *especially* those he misspelled, were his own.

Manzano's life and work illustrate what a humiliating experience slavery was. Both Guillén and Morejón have tried to depict this same humiliation in retrospect and correct the misconceptions and distortions of slave history. The approaches Guillén took at times were ground breaking as he found new ways to tell the old stories. The search for the intimate history of the Black slave is evident in the poetry of Nancy Morejón, but so are the themes of courage, freedom, and perseverance; "Mujer negra," her epic poem, which recalls the Atlantic crossing like much of Guillén's work. The theme of slavery is prominent in Guillén's poetry as was Africa, both as ancestral past and violated history. As Keith Ellis has succinctly summarized:

> The variety of ways in which Guillén deals with slavery suggests that it is searingly painful to his imagination. It is treated in a parable of horror in "Balada del güije" ["Ballad of the River Spirit"], as blank past in "Llegada" ["Arrival"]. The victims are portrayed as white in *El diario que a diario,* and lethal violence affecting slave and slave master is shown in the poem "Ancestros" ["Ancestors"]. The slave driver's whip makes many appearances following its initial one in the "Balada de los dos abuelos" ["Ballad of the Two Grandfathers"]; the "Sangre en las espaldas del negro inicial" ["Blood on the back of the first black man"] is present in the "Elegía a Jacques Roumain" ["Elegy to Jacques Roumain"]; and the open sores caused by the whip are vividly displayed in "Noches de negros junto a la catedral" ["Night of Blacks next to the Cathedral"]. In "El apellido" ["The Family Name"] there is rage at the loss of an original identity.[15]

Black people everywhere owe a debt to Guillén because he was one of the first in this century, certainly in Cuba, to write about slavery, to speak out against racism, to insist on Black pride, and to bring a positive image of Blacks and Black culture to literature.

Guillén approached Black slave history from many angles in his poetry, always trying to see the positive message that the very fact of Black survival has for those of us who still have to combat, as he himself had to do, slavery's negative legacy. Whatever else it does, Guillén's poetry urges us to remember the past and teaches us how to overcome

that legacy. I believe that the key to Guillén's significance for Black people lies precisely in his poems on slavery because they effectively convey
how Black people feel or should feel. Such poems as "Yo vine en un
barco negrero" ["I Came on a Slave Ship," II, 106] "Llegada" ["Arrival,"
I, 115] and "El apellido" ["My Last Name," I, 394] in particular as well
as others, among them "Son número 6" ["*Son* Number 6," I, 231] and
"La voz esperanzada" ["The Hopeful Voice," I, 215], conjure up timeless
qualities of resilience and pride, and they tell the Black epic story in the
first person. Over a decade ago, Luis F. González-Cruz noted that reality
in Guillén's poetry is seen "as if vicariously experienced by the black
man he partially is."[16] González-Cruz's point is that Guillén's work,
unlike *negrista* poetry by non-Black writers, presents a Black reality to
the reader that was directly felt by the author.

This personal attachment gave Guillén license to shake Black pride
into the subject of "Sabás" (I, 140) and to hurl insults in *Motivos de son* as
challenges designed to make Blacks think about themselves in a positive
way. Guillén was a mulatto but was Black enough to have lived, as he
once said, "mi tragedia de ser negro" [my tragedy of being Black]. Guillén's "Vine en un barco nergrero" is about Black Cuban history, but the
poetic "I" of the poem fuses with the entire Black race and speaks for all
those who came to the New World on a slave ship. His "Llegada" is a
celebration of Black contribution, pride, and determination, ancient
qualities also celebrated in "El apellido," Guillén's poem that, like
Hughes's "The Negro Speaks of Rivers" takes us back to ancient roots,
way back to before his "new" name was given him.

Keith Ellis has likened "El apellido" to Neruda's *Alturas de Macchu
Picchu* [*The Heights of Macchu Picchu*] in that both poets search for a people's roots (Ellis, 121). But Ellis correctly states, as did González-Cruz
before him, that Guillén as speaker is more involved in the experience he
conveys, which is why it is easy for Black readers to be involved in that
same experience. In this "family elegy" on the death of a name (and by
extension, identity), Guillén reaches out to all Blacks who share the
same ancestral history and loss. By reading the lines "Yo soy también el
nieto / biznieto, / tataranieto de un esclavo" [I am also the grandson, /
great-grandson, / great-great-grandson of a slave; I, 397], we know he
is talking not just about loss of identity and name but also about survival in America, about the pain associated with that survival, and about
the length of time that Blacks have had to endure it.

Guillén wrote many poems on slavery, "Sudor y látigo" ["Sweat and
Lash," I, 227], for example, but as Ellis has indicated in the passage

above, it is in *El diario que a diario* (1972) where the poet, by making his slaves White, turns to the theme of slavery with a significant difference. Guillén is the master of the *son* poem as evident in *Motivos de son* and other works, but he is also a master innovator in long poetry as well, and *El diario que a diario* is one of his longest. *El diario* has been characterized as "a poem posing as a newspaper posing as a chronicle,"[17] but we should add that what it is not—an epic poem—is also important. In fact, Guillén was the first to say so; in the introduction to *El diario,* he writes, "In order not to write either a textbook or an epic poem I used a series of scenes. . . ."[18] His stated intention is to suggest the indignities associated with Black slavery by making his slaves White.

Guillén decided not to write an epic poem perhaps because he believed the country's history prior to Castro lent itself more to parody and satire. Besides, he had already celebrated in epic fashion the heroic story of the revolution, for example, in the "Romancero" section of *Tengo* [*I Have,* 1964], which has Fidel Castro as the central presence in a series of five historical romances, "the verse form of the ancient Spanish epics" (Ellis, 149). *El diario* is not itself a parody of Cuban history. Rather, it presents the parody that Cuban history was, in Guillén's view, before the revolution, which was its inevitable and necessary result. He does this in a form appropriate to his unheroic subject. The anti-epic nature of El diario is heightened by the inclusion of the "heroic" poem "De esa manera" ["This way"], which in fragmented fashion frames the periods of domination that characterize Cuban history. Guillén published this poem separately, Augier tells us, in October 1968 in commemoration of the centenary of the beginning of the first war of independence begun by Carlos Manuel de Cespedes, an event Augier believes began a 100-year-long struggle and revolutionary tradition in Cuba.[19]

This interpolated poem, together with references to such Cuban heroes as Antonio Maceo, Juan Gualberto Gómez, José Martí, and (obliquely) Fidel Castro, stands in sharp contrast to the shameful history that Guillén presents in the rest of *El diario que a diario.* Black slavery was perhaps the most shameful part of that history. At first glance the most striking feature of Guillén's chronicle is the almost total absence of direct reference to Black slaves and slavery. This is not to say that they are unrepresented; they are obliquely and cleverly present. We could even say that the virtual absence of Black slave history in the work makes us more acutely aware of its presence because the reader is left wondering about it, especially in the section devoted entirely to "Esclavos europeos" ["European Slaves" II, 375–79]. In this section, whose time frame falls during the period of the Spanish conquest and occupation, Guillén, through an ultimate act of reversal, makes all of these slaves White but uses terminology clearly designed to evoke the Black slave experience in Cuba.

Vera Kutzinski is right to say that these conspicuous distortions, which completely reverse historical roles, create considerable confusion in the mind of the reader, who has been historically conditioned to think of slaves exclusively as Black (Kutzinski 1987, 189). In this section, White slaves appear in several advertisements and announcements; girls, men, children, couples, the whole gamut of human merchandise here are all White.[20] When Guillén talks about a White youngster for sale, however, we know he is not talking about White slaves at all. White slaves did exist, but few of today's readers know this. Guillén places White slaves in this work not to educate the public on this point but to raise White consciousness about the repulsive nature of Black slavery, which everybody does know about. The expectation of finding Black slaves in *El diario que a diario* makes this reversal work, whether or not White slaves existed. This strategy is not used here to show that White slavery was as bad as Black slavery or that slavery is bad whatever the color of those enslaved but simply to catch the reader off guard, to capture the attention and make him or her think. By making his slaves White, Guillén is not only attacking the repulsive nature of slavery but contemporary reader complacency as well. Guillén also reversed roles so that White people could better relate to the degradation normally associated with slavery and thus gain a new and unsettling perspective on the history of Black slavery in Cuba. This element of shock helps make *El diario que a diario* worthwhile reading and a valuable addition to the Hispanic canon.

Slavery is ever present in Guillén's work because its legacy reaches into the present. This legacy, as manifest in the contemporary Black world in Cuba, was his motivation to write and publish *Motivos de son*. In these early poems, which have been called, among other things, love poems (Ellis, 66) and baroque minidramas,[21] Guillén explored a variety of issues that continue to plague the Black community, from hunger, unemployment, and poverty to racial jealousies between Blacks and mulattos.

It is true, as Vera Kutzinski shows, that the *mulata* emerged from nineteenth-century "discursive entwinements" (Kutzinski 1993, 13) as a product of mostly White male desire to become an attractive sexual object in the "masculine poetics" of twentieth-century Afro-Cubanism.

Yet one of the lasting impressions I get from reading *Motivos de son* is the preference of the *negro bembón* [big-lipped Black] for his *negra*. The pride in Blackness expressed in these poems partly explains why the starting point for Guillén's lasting fame and for his canonization begins with this small collection. I believe Guillén will be remembered for *Motivos de son,* for his poems on slavery, and for such lengthy works as *El diario que a diario,* but other critics, most recently Ian Smart, J. Kubayanda, and Clement White, have staked out their positions, too. Smart's book on Nicolás Guillén is different from others on the Afro-Cuban poet, and he tells us so himself in the concluding chapter: "I attempt to appreciate Guillén, the Caribbean poet, on the basis of an indigenous literary theory, and this approach contradicts those of other books on Guillén" (Smart, 163). This difference is the most interesting aspect of Smart's book; whereas Kubayanda focuses on African values and African-inspired language in Guillén's poetry, Smart's work is, in essence, a book on Caribbean poetics and plants Guillén squarely in the West Indian literary tradition by stressing linkages among Black poetic oral forms found around the Caribbean.

In the poetics of West Indianness, Smart sees Guillén's *El son entero* [*The Complete* Son], for example, as precursor and analogous to "The Complete Reggae." He also defines Guillén's humor in *El diario que a diario* as West Indian but with ties to Africa and to the tradition of the trickster figure. Smart even goes further back to Egypt for some of his interpretations, but to Kubayanda it is the concept of drum poetics that is central. Also, although Smart characterizes Vera Kutzinski's *Against the American Grain* as brilliant in seeing the "carnivalesque" nature of Guillén's work, Kubayanda is less charitable, attacking her "Eurocentric revisionism" and the "collective misreadings" she and her co-contributors give to Guillén's poetry in *Nicolás Guillén: A Special Issue* (*Callaloo* 10, no. 2 [1987]), which Kutzinski edited. Smart and Kubayanda have their differences, but in the final analysis neither sees Guillén's poetry limited by natural boundaries or dominated by Europe. White rejects what he considers misguided assumptions about Guillén in his attempt to "decode" the Afro-Cuban poet's message, which is pro-Black and antiracist.

With the passing of Nicolás Guillén in 1989, Nancy Morejón became Cuba's new Black canonical star.[22] Morejón looks back to slavery as Guillén did, but she also looks within and tries to recreate the intimate history of the Black slave woman. Elizabeth Fox-Genovese chose the quotation "Slavery is terrible for men, but it is far more terrible for women" in a recent discussion of the burdens, wrongs, and suffering that slave women endured.[23] These words call to mind Morejón, who wrote "Mujer negra" in an attempt to reconstruct through an epic, first-person voice a part of Cuban history, namely, the story of the Black women of her country, and in this she has succeeded admirably. Her female voice helps make this Afro-Cuban group pivotal because it complements very well Manzano's original voice and the "sublime masculinity" (Kutzinski 1993, 163–98) of Guillén. The kind of woman we see in "Mujer negra" does not appear in such a specific way in Guillén's poetry, and the absence of such a female presence in his key poems on Black history is one of Kutzinski's complaints. What is most interesting about Morejón's poem, however, is Linda Howe's recent interpretation of it as a vehicle for the poet who speaks through the historical Black female slave but for a contemporary purpose,[24] not unlike the one that Vera Kutzinski reads into Guillén's *El diario que a diario.*

Both Howe and Kutzinski raise the contemporary question: Did Guillén and Morejón toe the party line in the late 1970s and early 1980s, or did they subvert it? If we believe G. Cabrera Infante, Nicolás Guillén was a proud mulatto right up to the end who once called Fidel Castro a "son of a bitch" and a "gangster."[25] This disaffection gains currency if we accept Kutzinski's view that *El diario que a diario* reflects Guillén's resistance to authority. To her, Guillén's "posture of resistance" (Kutzinski 1987, 235) in this work, which she sees as a highly literate subversion, does not suggest a favorable ideological bent toward Castro and his revolution. Kutzinski's argument is that contrary to popular opinion, Guillén never ceased being an Afro-American poet after the revolution. The publication date of *El diario que a diario* (1972) becomes significant when we relate this work to the point that Linda Howe makes regarding Nancy Morejón's "Mujer negra." Basing her interpretation on information provided by Carlos Moore's book,[26] she believes that "Mujer negra" was Morejón's response specifically to Castro's crackdown on ethnic grievances in 1968 and on Black Power movements in Cuba following the "Turbulent Sixties." Moore wrote that Morejón had been silenced or suppressed, but Howe's view is that Morejón managed to subvert the process through "Mujer negra" and later through "Amo a mi Amo" {"I Love My Master," 1979}, stating her case for Blackness while at the same time accepting and criticizing the political imperative. If Kutzinski is right, perhaps Guillén did the same in *El diario,* which would have both Morejón and Guillén making anti-Castro statements, with Morejón in particular defending Blackness and the

Black woman because of unwanted censorship. These new readings of their poetry show dissenting opinions in politically accepted works that disguise true intent.[27]

"Mujer negra" appeared in book form in 1979 in *Parajes de una época*[28] [*Parameters of an Epoch*] but was first published in 1975 in *Casa de las Americas*.[29] In subsequent books it often reappears grouped with such other slave-oriented poems as "Amo a mi amo." Howe's analysis classifying "Mujer negra" as a "double discourse" that is only partly about Afro-Cuban women in the Latin America slavery system but is largely a reaction to and product of the political struggle with the Castro regime over Black consciousness is interesting because this poem and "Amo a mi amo," which first appeared in book format in the 1982 publication *Octubre imprescindible* [*Indispensable October*], speaks both to the reality of past slavery and symbolically to current racism. Either way, "Mujer negra" represents definitively the Black woman's perspective in intimate and rebellious detail that is absent from both Manzano's *Autobiografía* and Guillén's poems on slavery.

Morejón, like Guillén, is a poetic spokesperson claimed by Blacks, apologists for Castro's Cuba, and crusaders for the Third World. In addition, as a Cuban Black woman writer she is lionized by feminists who are interested in women writers in general. Morejón once said that for the most part she does not write intentionally as a feminist or specifically as a Black woman, but it is easy to see why Black and female readers identify with her poetry. Nancy Morejón is indeed the "new woman" of Cuba, but recent criticism on this point is not uniform because it is not clear just what that means in Cuba today. Claudette Rose Green-Williams, for example, sees irony in the title of Morejón's poem "Mujer negra."[30] She believes that the racial specificity it anticipates is undercut by the raceless nationalism that she believes the poem espouses. This means, in her view, that Morejón has allowed complicity with official revolutionary ideology to override both her Black and feminist consciousness. This reading, of course, conflicts with that of Linda Howe, who, by seeing the poem as a reaction not just to the past but to contemporary racial politics in Cuba as well, puts an entirely new spin on the Cuban author's work in general and on "Mujer negra" in particular. Miriam de Costa Willis has argued, as have others, that an examination of Morejón's poetry reveals that Morejón has both a strong racial awareness and a well-developed feminist consciousness and that such poems as "Mujer negra" underscore rather than detract from the sexual and the racial dimensions of Cuban nationalism.[31] She believes, as I do, that first and foremost Morejón is committed to the revolutionary ideals of the new Cuba even when she finds herself at odds with the people who now run the country. In any event her poems, taken overall, do reflect her "feminism" and her ethnicity.

In this chapter I have talked about how pivotal these three Afro-Cubans are. Yet I should point out that there is a recent book called *AfroCuba: An Anthology of Cuban Writing on Race, Politics and Culture,* edited by Pedro Pérez Sarduy and Jean Stubbs (Melbourne: Ocean Press, 1993), in which Manzano, curiously, is only mentioned once despite what it says in the appendix, and other than an excerpt from Morejón's *Nación y mestizaje en Nicolás Guillén (Nation and Race Mixing in Nicolás Guillen;* Havana: UNEAC, 1982), neither the poetry of Guillén nor of Morejón is highlighted. This underrepresentation suggests something artificial about a book called *AfroCuba.*³² Also curious is the authors' decision not to identify writers by race. Their explanation: *White* Cuban contributors might object if wrongly identified. José Martí's famous words, "There can be no racial hate because there are no races," which Kutzinski calls high minded and well intentioned (Kutzinski 1993, 6), sound good, but the attempt over the years to "deracialize" Cuba has not worked. This new anthology of Cuban writings on race, politics, and culture seems to be the latest attempt.

AfroCuba, in part, is a response to Carlos Moore's earlier, well-known work that inspired much of Howe's interpretation of Morejón's "Mujer negra." Like Cabrera Infante, Moore is extremely critical of Castro's Cuba, leaving the impression (among many others) that not just Morejón but Guillén as well had been repressed. Moore's work, more than any other, gave rise to the speculation that the poetry and the politics of these two prominent Afro-Cubans were altered and certainly affected by the heavy-handed treatment of Cuban authorities. The editors of *AfroCuba* dismiss Moore as a Cuban out of the country and out of touch, but the current unsettled situation in Cuba does seem to be bringing the race issue more in focus to the outside world.

Cutting through all of the posturing and politics, Ingrid Peritz's recent report reveals that in Cuba today, the legacy of slavery is still very real.³³ On the surface Cuba is an integrationist's dream, but ingrained racism, she writes, still runs deep in the country. The gist of her report is that even if Cuba under Castro officially became color-blind, many Whites did not, and that while racism did not end under Castro's rule, talking about racism did. In fact, one of her informants tells her that anti-Black sentiment is growing as Cubans endure widespread hardships because people are looking for a scapegoat. Her informants, as well as the editors of *AfroCuba* and Moore, however, do seem to agree on one thing: that the return of the predominantly White Cubans from Miami would pose a serious threat to whatever gains Black Cubans have made since slavery and certainly over the past 35 years.

Chapter Four

Miscegenation and Personal Choice in Venezuela: Message and *Mestizaje* in Juan Pablo Sojo's *Nochebuena negra*

Ce qui caractérise le peuple vénézuelien, c'est son profond métissage. [What characterizes the Venezuelan people is their deep-seated racial mixture.]

Maurice Belrose

Venezuela prides itself on being one of the most miscegenated countries in South America.

Marvin Lewis

Miscegenation, or race mixing, exists in Latin America, but *mestizaje,* as the process is called in Spanish, has always been a contentious component of identity. Interracial attraction, both willing and forced, has been the hallmark of *mestizo* America. Yet when it comes to having Black blood, admitting to it for some is easier when it does not show. Also, for many who live in the countries where the term applies, *mestizaje* is something that happens to others or should not happen at all. Venezuela prides itself on being one of the most miscegenated countries in South America, as Marvin Lewis has written,[1] but one Afro-Venezuelan writer, Juan Pablo Sojo, expresses some mixed feelings about the process and its acceptance in his country. Miscegenation is indeed the primary unifying thematic motif of Sojo's novel, *Nochebuena negra* [*Black St. John's Eve*], but even though Sojo recognized that at least the majority of Venezuelans have something of Blackness, he also knew that the prejudice based on skin color "painfully paralyzes our national life" (Lewis, 9). Sojo, who died in 1948, tried to reconcile these two seemingly contrasting realities first in *Nochebuena negra*[2] and later in his book of essays *Temas y apuntes afro-venezolanos*[3] [*Afro-Venezuelan Themes and Notes,* 1943]. Born in 1908,

35

Sojo wrote his novel in 1930 at the age of 22 and published it 13 years later, in 1943, the same year in which his book of essays was published.

Most, if not all, Black Hispanic writers at one time or another deal with the issue of *mestizaje*. How they come to terms with this reality in their own lives and in their literature has provided, as I indicated in the first chapter, challenges for them as writers and for us as readers, especially those of us who are Black North American critics accustomed to thinking Black and seeing racism where it exists. I have found that the "Blacker" the work, the more complex the treatment of *mestizaje,* and this has been true from the time of Manzano up through the present and especially so in such twentieth-century works as Adalberto Ortiz's *Juyungo* and Sojo's *Nochebuena negra*. Not many countries' writers have more written about the Black theme than those in Venezuela, though entire books on the subject have been published with no mention at all of him. This is unfortunate because few have contributed as much on this theme or wrestled more valiantly with the pain of prejudice in his country than he. In fact, Juan Pablo Sojo, like Nicomedes Santa Cruz, was for a long time seen as the lone Black voice speaking for Venezuela, a status that increases the value of what he has to say especially on a topic as vital to that nation as miscegenation.

Nochebuena negra is overridden with Black culture, customs, music, and dance as well as the general experiences and hardships that come with living in a Black skin, but when interracial relationships—and there are several in the novel—become part of the mix, how the author treats them tells us something about his views on *mestizaje* in his country. The complexity arises and resolves itself when we look at both the practice (the novel) and the theory (the essays). Both levels of discourse relate to the question of personal choice, which seems to interest Sojo as it did me years ago in a study of Rómulo Gallego's *Pobre negro* [*Poor Black*] and Enrique López Albújar's *Matalaché.*[4] Like *Nochebuena negra,* these two novels deal in part with the irresistible attraction of the sexes across racial lines but, unlike Sojo's novel, they are set in another time and feature mulatto protagonists. Sojo's novel is different because he is not interested, as was Gallegos, in the vacillating mulatto, the mulatto's role in the future of Venezuela, or the mulatto as obstacle to progress or as symbol. In his novel Sojo presents several interracial relationships, but prejudice keeps the main interracial couple apart. By going this route, Sojo tells us that race mixing was an inevitable fact of Venezuelan life. However, while Gallegos posits an interracial future and a reconciliation from a vantage point in the past, Sojo addresses the issue by questioning the obstacle that prejudice presents in the present.

Nochebuena negra focuses on the difficulties of life for the farm laborers who worked the Pozo Frío cacao plantation from the turn of the century to the present; it is also a sensual, even erotic novel whose interracial relationships are used by the author to explore racial clichés between Black men and White women and between White men and Black women. One of the Black characters, Tereso, goes to the big city (Caracas), marries a "White" woman, Ana Rafaela, not from the area, and brings her back to the rural plantation he calls home. They leave when their life is made difficult. Sojo makes Tereso's objectives, which were initially suspect, quite plain: He has married her to improve the race: "Usté comprende, el colorcito. . . . Hay que mejorarlo, vale" (*NN,* 276). [You understand, it's the color thing. . . . One has to improve it, right?]. The reception accorded his wife by the locals is unwelcoming partly because he flaunts her and arouses jealousies. Ana Rafaela's presence enables Sojo to call up the desire of some Black men for White women not just to "improve the race" but their own station as well. Relationships ostensibly less controversial and therefore more acceptable between White men and Black women also exist in the novel, especially between Luis Pantoja and countless Black women on the plantation.

The relationship between Consuelo and Pedro seems possible but is thwarted not because Pedro is unwilling, as I once thought,[5] but because of social and racial forces outside himself. Pedro initially does indeed resist the "deseo que muerde a todo negro: tener mujer blanca" (*NN,* 236) [desire that eats away at every black: to have a white woman], and in this sense the contrast with Tereso who, unlike Pedro, aspired to be White, is made paramount. The temptation to link Pedro and Consuelo by a force "superior a la voluntad, los arrojó el uno contra el otro" (*NN,* 304) [stronger than their own will] exists but in the final analysis is rejected by the author, and this sets his novel, and Pedro and Consuelo in particular, apart from Gallegos's *Pobre negro,* in which the mulatto Pedro Miguel and the White Luisiana unite symbolically. This union, Gallegos makes dogmatically clear, augured well for the future of race relations in Venezuela. Sojo, however, muddies the water when he rejects a similarly rosy scenario for his star interracial couple. Pedro is clearly the author's mouthpiece, and Consuelo is obviously the liberal White voice. Bringing these two together only to separate them carries its own message on the key questions of *mestizaje* and prejudice.

With his emphasis on the wrong values Tereso, an example of misguided motivation, is the pathetic opposite of Pedro, an attractive,
intelligent, socially conscious sophisticated Black gentleman who
never loses sight of himself or his mission. Pedro did not want to be
just another *peón,* so got himself off the plantation and away from the
life of perpetual peonage. He became educated and returned to raise
awareness, as he had raised his own, and to use his new arsenal of
knowledge to help others. Pedro has big-city exposure as well as roots
in the region, but he does not get the girl because her White, upper-
class family sends her away and out of his reach. Personal choice is evident in Consuelo's opting for Pedro, but when Sojo depicts them as
casualties of prejudice, he sends the message that personal choice or
interracial love is not the problem but that coming to terms with them
is. After Consuelo is sent away, Pedro goes back to the big city but
returns and rededicates himself to redeeming his people. By novel's
end, Pedro has gotten Consuelo out of his thoughts, but the prejudice
that kept them apart still exists. Gallegos was writing about the past
and (optimistically) the future, but Sojo's novel, which is pessimistic
on this subject, faces up to the prejudice current in his time that was
an obstacle to positive change.

We could say that Sojo writes Consuelo out of Pedro's life so that
Pedro can carry on in the role of messiah to his people unencumbered by
their relationship, but I believe that Sojo has it fail to better highlight
the backward practice of prejudice that he sets out to expose. Pedro's
attraction to Consuelo was not a distraction from his commitment to
Blackness but rather one more manifestation of it, because freedom
should be part of that redemption; tolerance, personal choice, and gen-
uine acceptance as opposed to rhetoric are keys to the future as Sojo sees
it. Whatever else Pedro does as a redeemer of Blacks, his work is not
complete and the country not wholly distanced from its feudal and
racist past until he and others like him can move beyond symbol and
stereotype and have their own personal choice respected in all matters,
including those of the heart. Consuelo and Pedro are drawn to each
other for the right reasons, their relationship growing out of decent
intentions and mutual respect rather than racial and sexual mythology.
Although Pedro is initially suspicious of Consuelo, she wins him over. In
Pedro and Consuelo we see none of the artificial reasons that bring people together, only what keeps them apart, through which we see clearly
Sojo's message: Prejudice prevails. Miscegenation in Venezuela, if Sojo's
treatment of the aborted relationship between Pedro and Consuelo is an

example, is indeed "a one-way street controlled and dominated by the white male progenitor" (Lewis, 18).

Sojo is on record acknowledging that racial fusion happened more quickly and was more widespread in Venezuela than anywhere else in the Americas, that for whatever reasons the Spaniards who came to Venezuela coveted Black and Indian women despite the rigidity of the class structure (*Temas,* 11). He is clearly aware of the history of *mestizaje* in Venezuela and he writes at length about the process in his essays. In his novel Sojo shows some of the sexual liberties that overbearing landowners take with Black women. He even acknowledges that pure Blacks, except around the cacao plantations on the coast, are hard to find and that racial integration took place in Venezuela over time after slavery was abolished there in 1852 (*Temas,* 22–23). When he writes about the "Black" problem, he does not single out Venezuela as an exception; what happens in Venezuela is not unlike what happens in other parts of the world. The unique thing about Venezuela, he writes, is how Blackness manifests itself more in Venezuelan thought and customs than in how people look, although all the races are mixed up to some degree, especially in his country.

Because of all of this, Sojo finds prejudice based on skin color to be nonsensical. Nothing holds back progress more than prejudice, and he argues against it both in his novel and in his essays, where he addresses the problem directly and insists that the prejudice Whites feel toward Blacks has no place in the civilized societies all democracies claim to be. He points to the Hitlerism rampant during his time to illustrate the consequences that hatred based on race can have. He is adamant that there is no possible justification for racial prejudice on any grounds.

Sojo's categorical rejection of prejudice is consistent with the key message in *Nochebuena negra,* which is that prejudice, together with its ramifications, is an impediment not only to personal choice but to cultural progress. Sojo hopes the day is not far off when some world court will lay to rest the problem of prejudice once and for all. He also outlines the musical and artistic contribution that Blacks have made to Western culture despite their having toiled mightily, as they do in *Nochebuena negra.* The underlying message in these essays is clear: Slavery was abolished, but now prejudice based on race and color must be as well if Venezuela is to mean something of value in the family of nations.

Sojo's message in *Nochebuena negra* is a difficult one to sell because he exposes prejudice while at the same time acknowledging the reality of race mixing in Venezuela, which many take to suggest the existence and practice of a racial democracy. He does not walk this thin line as well in his essays as he does in his novel. The failed relationship of the two principal characters of *Nochebuena negra* speaks volumes on both interracial attraction and prejudice. However, Marvin Lewis correctly points out the perceived contradiction in Sojo's *Temas,* in which the author tries to downplay the presence of racism in his country by qualifying the kind of racial integration that has taken place there over the centuries. In explaining the historical process in Venezuela and the Black contribution to it, Sojo does not want to admit that the record on race in Venezuela is as bad as that of the United States or Nazi Germany, and he tries to set Venezuela apart by stating that Venezuelan prejudice in any event differs from other countries," limited as it is to color prejudice. Sojo does seem to flay about on the subject of *mestizaje* in his essays but not in *Nochebuena negra,* where he brings Pedro and Consuelo together and then keeps them apart.

In *Temas* Sojo emphasizes cultural over biological *mestizaje.* The latter did take place, however, and Sojo knows it, as his novel shows and as he tells us in his essays. Black Venezuelans did bring color, hair, and features to the mix as much as anything else but Sojo fine-tunes his presentation by telling us on the one hand that such manifestations of biological *mestizaje* do not show up as much as other manifestations of Black culture that all Venezuelans have internalized and on the the other that racial purity does not exist in Venezuela or anywhere else. Sojo's splitting hairs over varieties of *mestizaje* should not detract, however, from his argument against the continuing practice of prejudice. The task Sojo set for himself as a Black writer in a *mestizo* society was not an easy one, and thus the necessary attention to the complexities of these issues.

In his study, Lewis called *Nochebuena negra* a landmark novel, characterizing it as the most important fictional affirmation of Black culture published to date in Venezuela, and he is right. He also discusses other works, including Ramón Díaz Sánchez's *Cumboto,* and that author's literary interpretation of miscegenation as a national practice designed to whiten Blacks out of existence. Lewis's work is a welcome new contribution, especially his fair analysis of Sojo's difficulty in adhering to the school of thought set forth in dominant Venezuelan social ideology that regards being Black in Venezuela as nonproblematic. Sojo knew that there was a pigmentocracy in his country. In his analysis of *Temas,* Lewis highlights Sojo's hesitancy in admitting that color/ethnicity was the most important inhibitor to Black progress in Venezuela. Theoretically, Venezuelans are not judged by the color of their skin, Sojo tells us in his essays, but he clearly knew this not to be the case and had to admit it. Sojo's dilemma is one more manifestation of the complexity of complexion in Latin America.

Lewis raises two important questions: How are Sojo's contradictory attitudes integrated into his work of fiction? And is there consistence in Sojo's worldview? I have tried to answer these questions by focusing on the role of Pedro and Consuelo in *Nochebuena negra,* where the author brings personal choice into the equation. As Lewis perceptively points out, there is no evidence that a sexual union between Consuelo and Pedro is consummated (Lewis, 18). If we accept that Ana Rafaela technically is a light-skinned Indian seen as White, then there is no sexual union at all between a Black man and a White woman in Sojo's novel. For these reasons, by making personal choice the real casualty in his fictional treatment of race relations, Sojo finds a way to comment critically not just on miscegenation but also on the widespread prejudice he saw as equally pervasive in his country.

Sojo explores many aspects of the Black experience in the Barlovento region of Venezuela. The novel is especially useful for those who wish to examine how the Black characters interact with White landowners who control the power and consequently play dominant roles in their social, economic, and personal lives. The novel is also invaluable for the light it sheds on Sojo's grasp of Black folklore, anthropology, and ritual practices and of the machinations of the rich and powerful. *Nochebuena negra,* however, brings more to the Hispanic canon than a Black perspective on social protest, magic realism, and Afro-Venezuelan drum culture. There are some fine episodes depicting all of this, but what Sojo's novel especially brings is sensitivity in its treatment of an interracial relationship that had no chance. This failure, more than anything else in the novel, magnifies Venezuela's true problem as Sojo saw it. In his fictional world there really is no contradiction at all.

Chapter Five

Ambiguity, *locura*, and Black Ambition in Two Afro-Ecuadorian Novels: Adalberto Ortiz's *Juyungo* and Nelson Estupiñán Bass's *El último río*

I was stupid. . . . I recognize that I was an imbecile, but you're still one.
José Antonio Pastrana in *El último río*

Adalberto Ortiz, who already has been canonized in the Afro-Hispanic field, has written several works of poetry and prose over the past 50 years. However, his first novel, *Juyungo* (1943), will always be considered not only his most representative work but also the prototypical novel on the Black experience in Latin America. This "black Ecuadorian classic,"[1] now available in English,[2] deserves wider recognition because it touches so many social, racial, literary, and psychological bases of interest to readers on race in Latin America. The novel's impact ranges from the solid portrayal of Ascensión Lastre (Juyungo), a heroic, Black protagonist, to the depiction of ambivalence on race, class, and color in Ecuador. Juyungo does not know about Black history, but he is nevertheless a memorable creation for the most part because of his own "modern black heroism."[3]

Nelson Estupiñán Bass, Ortiz's compatriot, has given us another memorable Black Ecuadorian character, José Antonio Pastrana, in *El último río* (1966). For his role in this novel, also available in English,[4] Pastrana deserves recognition as one of the most controversial characters in Black Hispanic literature largely, as we shall see, because of his treatment of Blacks and women. In recent years Estupiñán Bass has been more productive than Ortiz and, in his later works, more experimental than his Afro-Ecuadorian colleague as well. I believe, however, that

42

Estupiñán Bass's lasting fame, for our purposes, will come to rest on *El último río,* which is perhaps his best work.

Both *Juyungo* and *El último río* open doors into the Black psyche, but what we find there should be clearly understood by the reader because the psychology of Blacks is nowhere presented in a more ambiguous, complex, and powerful manner than in these two novels. Both Ortiz and Estupiñán Bass immerse the reader in one way or another in the race issue, whose complexities they explore in new and different ways. What clouds Ortiz's message is that in his work, race intertwines with the class issue, whereas in Estupiñán Bass's novel the relationship between race and ambition is taken to new and dizzying heights.

Both authors take us inside the minds of their characters, but this is not unusual for Black Hispanic authors to do. Levels of ambiguity confront us, as we shall see in a later chapter, in Duncan's *Los cuatro espejos* (1973), for example, and Zapata Olivella also has a great deal of reconciliation on race to do in *¡Levántate mulato!,* his autobiographical account that I discuss in the next chapter. The task of interpretation becomes more treacherous for the reader of *Juyungo* and *El último río,* however, because these two works seem to belie the authors' apparent intent. In Ortiz's novel "class more than race" is the author's oft-repeated motif, but as we look closer, we see that Juyungo's much touted "thirst" for justice has less to do with social class than with a man acting heroically out of his own pride in himself and his lineage. Estupiñán Bass, both in his novel and in conversations about it, points to ruthless ambition as his character's main flaw. Pastrana's "thirst" is for power, but I believe that this ambition turns out to be not just his flaw but his salvation.

These two Afro-Ecuadorian novels have their differences. But I am interested here in their most obvious similarity, which is that both novels are grounded in acts of *locura* (madness) by dominant protagonists who derive strength for all their actions from their self-definition as Black macho males. Their paths and methods of expression are clearly different, but they are really two sides of the same coin: Both are Blacks who hate the stigma imposed on them by White racism. The concept of self-worth, while easy to monitor in *Juyungo's* Ascensión Lastre, is often lost on readers of *El último río* who dismiss Pastrana as a "consummate jackass, a negrophobic Negro," as Ian Smart phrases it, who takes the self-hatred "that afflicts African-ancestored people to new levels of lunacy" (*River,* back cover). Though I once dismissed Pastrana as "an antihero, a 'white puppet' who obtains the support of whites and the wrath of blacks" (Jackson 1988, 42), I do not now believe that Pastrana's self-hatred is as important as his hatred of how Blackness—his and others'—is perceived. For a time he also hates other Blacks who do not declare or believe themselves to be equal to Whites.

Pastrana never doubts or denies his own self-worth, which is why we should not lose sight of the White (not Black) racism that impacts so heavily on him that he is driven to the lunacy of trying to give the impression that he thinks he is White. His goal is to acquire White power, or to wield power the way White people do; along the way he covets positions of power normally reserved for Whites and also covets White women with whom he hopes to have White children. Pastrana literally forces his Black self on a society that prizes and rewards Whiteness. In *Juyungo,* Ascensión's final act of Black macho *locura* brings that novel to its ambiguous conclusion. Pastrana displays his own kind of *locura* in *El último río,* and his lunacy contributes to an ambiguity that becomes more pronounced when we are privy to Pastrana's inner thoughts. These thoughts are more extensive in the first edition of the novel that Estupiñán Bass published in 1966[5] than in subsequent editions, in which much of Pastrana's paranoiac ramblings have been trimmed. Both in this first edition and in subsequent ones, however, the constant encouragement of his "yo interior" [inner voice] keeps his confidence strong with such lines as "Shit, I'm a macho man" and "It's not everyone who can take the hundred and fifty lashes" (*River,* 37), which he is forced to do at one defining moment in the novel.

El último río has been read as a political metaphor for the failure of liberalism in Ecuador[6] and as a love story (a "battle of the sexes"[7]) ending with Pastrana, now old, suffering the "desencanto" [disenchantment] of a "complejo de inferioridad" [inferiority complex] toward his young wife, Ana Mercedes.[8] This inadequacy—which is not racial—is brought about not so much by the impotence of old age as by a broader awareness of all the positive things she represents. Ana Mercedes is the "last river" of the title.[9] The novel, in large measure, is her story, too, "written" by Jose Antonio Pastrana—who left notes—and published by Juan, a narrator of but also a participant in the story. The author's narrative strategies, which Henry Richards has discussed,[10] ennoble Estupiñán Bass's artistic effort, and the portrayal of the romantic, political, and business passions that drive Pastrana are central to the novel's success. But more than anything else *El último río,* like *Juyungo,* is a novel about race. In both of these novels the black protagonists will themselves the physical and mental strength to overcome the obstacles that racism presents. Estupiñán Bass has confided that Pastrana is a composite character based on some Black types he has observed, namely, Blacks who "think" they are White and who exploit other Blacks (Richards 1991, 22). His obvious message to Black readers is that they should beware of such individuals and not try to emulate them. The not-so-obvious message this novel carries to White readers is embodied in Pastrana as an adept example of role reversal—he is a "White" racist who is Black. Much of the ambiguity in this novel's message is wrapped up in this paradox.

Estupiñán Bass sets the stage for the ambiguous nature of his character's drive for power when he speaks of the "estrategias del amor" [love strategies] (Richards 1991, 22) that Pastrana uses to get his way. In reference to his character's "artimañas" [tricks], the author states

> La narrativa contemporánea ya no presenta el bueno bueno y el malo malo, ha borrado de sus cuartillas el maniqueísmo. Los narradores de hoy acuarelizamos los sujetos con sus lados, todos plausibles y abominables, en la búsqueda de equilibrios y desarticulaciones. Es decir, sin aquella sanidad o profilaxis que exhibía un sujeto sofisticado, desdeñando las anormalidades que en la vida tienen la inclinación a volverse normales. (Richards 1991, 27)

> [Contemporary narrative no longer presents the good good and the bad bad; it has taken Manichaeanism off its pages. We narrators today paint our subjects from all sides, all of them equally believable and abominable, in our search for balance and variety. We try to avoid those squeaky clean images because in life sometimes the abnormal turns out to be quite normal.]

Pastrana seems abnormal in the extreme because he goes to such great lengths to be successful. He turns custom upside down, and he does this by taking a position that his society deems to be quite normal, namely, that one has to be White to get anywhere. This racist thought would likely go unnoticed if uttered and practiced by someone White, but this idiocy seems absurd coming from a Black. Once held up to the scrutiny it demands, Pastrana's racism gives pause precisely because it is so abnormal.

When we apply this scrutiny to Pastrana, we see that he is more than simply a Black man struggling with the split personality of a divided self, an admission the author himself makes. In response to the question "Los monólogos interiores de José Pastrana revelan una condición esquizofrénica. ¿Está Ud. de acuerdo con esta idea?" [Do you agree that José Pastrana's interior monologues reveal a split personality?], Estupiñán Bass replies: "Antes que esquizofrénico, Pastrana es megalómano. En sus monólogos y en sus actitudes durante el tiempo de sus aberraciones, mantiene permanente cohesionada y coherente su manía de grandeza" (Richards 1991, 23) [Rather than schizophrenic, Pastrana is a megalomaniac. In his monologues and in his way of thinking during his period of aberrant behavior, his delusions of grandeur remained lucid, coherent, and intact]. Estupiñán Bass does indeed use Pastrana's character to strike a blow against greed and the unequal distribution of wealth. He makes this point in the novel when one of the Black characters observes: "It's not a racial struggle . . . but a struggle between those who have and want more and the humble folk. . . . Pastrana is against our race not because he's 'white' rather because he's rich" (*River,* 182). This is the author's larger message. Estupiñán Bass does not dwell on Pastrana's split personality, yet his desire to achieve wealth and power is clearly rooted in the prevailing mythology of his society, which is that Whiteness equals wholeness.[11] Pastrana's plan is to literally use stolen money to buy into that mythology, at least for a while. By doing so, however, he not only achieves wealth and power; he also forces White people who believe this mythology to take another look at it. This second look is inevitable because Pastrana is not just a crazy Black man who "thinks" he is White but one whose White racist rhetoric reflects their own grotesque views.

Pastrana's actions function as a ruse guaranteed to get White racism in Ecuador the scrutiny it deserves. We have seen this ruse elsewhere in Black hispanic literature. In Martín Morúa Delgado's late nineteenth-century novel *Sofía* (1891), a White girl lives what closely resembles a slave existence, and more recently in Nicolás Guillén's *El diario que a diario* (1972), the slave characters are White. In both cases these "slaves" would likely go unnoticed if they were Black because White readers would find nothing unusual about them. Making them White challenges the readers' complacency. The same thing happens in Nelson Estupiñán Bass's *El último río* but in reverse: A Black man spewing White racist hatred is an anomaly that cannot be ignored. Pastrana is indeed a caricature of a negrophobic Negro but, much like the exaggerated characters that Cubena developed in his *Los nietos de Felicidad Dolores,* he also serves as a mirror held up before Whites to reflect their racism back onto its source.

In *Juyungo,* Ascensión Lastre asserts himself through heroic acts worthy of the family name; his black uncle had established the tradition. In

El último río, Pastrana also considers himself to be a worthy Black man, but he derives strength from his own Black macho self while at the same time separating himself from his color by refusing to let society's negative assessment of it stand in his way. Curiously, Pastrana achieves in spite of his color and because of it as well. If he were not Black, he might not have had the same degree of ambition. His challenges are to make others accept him as they would a White person and believe the fiction he has so carefully fashioned, namely, that he thinks of himself as White.

Pastrana's saving grace is that he changes his mind about racism. When he says to a White employee who had been eager to carry out his foolish racist orders, "I was stupid. . . . I recognize that I was an imbecile, but you're still one" (*River,* 153), we arrive at the major alarm this novel sounds: Pastrana's racist period is short lived, but White racism is not. His farcical behavior and ridiculous anti-Black policies take center stage for a while, but he does come to his senses, while those around him do not. One message in this novel is that Blacks should be wary of negrophobic Negroes, but another is that Pastrana is in error. White people are not role models simply because their skin is white. A few years ago, when I first considered Pastrana to be a caricature of a Black man whose cult of Whiteness was so strong that he was able to convince himself for a time that he really was White, I indicated that Pastrana eventually arrives at the more balanced view that all people are equal.[12] My view now is that Pastrana actually starts out believing this but has to overcompensate with his ludicrous actions to get ahead. Part of this overcompensation involves convincing himself that he is "White on the inside," not in the sense of being a Black man with the proverbial White (noble) soul but of believing he had the same right to the privileged existence that White people enjoy. In his quest for a share of that privilege, Pastrana turns himself into a White racist with a Black face.

Pastrana's search is not really for identity because he knows who he is: not only a Black man but also a stubborn Black man, the "best" (*River,* 36). Like Ascensión Lastre in *Juyungo,* Pastrana has crossed a lot of rivers in his lifetime. He has met each affront, whether in wartime battle or civilian life, with "guts," the word his inner voice constantly uses to keep him primed. His delusion or strategy of Whiteness—convincing others to treat him as though he were white—has been the challenge of his life, especially because everybody—Black and White—thinks he was a fool. In fact, the phrase "Estos son otros José Antonio Pastrana" [They are acting like José Antonio Pastrana], according to Estupiñán Bass, has come to refer to Ecuadorian Blacks who act like Pastrana when they acquire riches, "cuando se hacen potentados" [when they become big shots].[13] The novel, as Estupiñán Bass often makes clear, is a criticism of such ambitious *negros potentados* who turn their backs on their own people once they get to the top. But Pastrana's extreme behavior is too exaggerated to be simply an attack on racial dualism.

El último río is a parody of Blacks who have mastered the art of White racism and greed toward Blacks. But we have to remember that Pastrana is not suffering from an inferiority complex but rather has a feeling of great confidence in himself and that during his crazy period, he has less confidence in other Blacks precisely because he has so much in himself. What Pastrana is also saying in the novel—and Nelson Estupiñán Bass has repeated it in an interview—is that although all people are equal, a Black person "si llega a cultura es superior tal vez al blanco" (Bolden, 26) [if he acquires culture is perhaps superior to Whites]. Pastrana convinces himself of the truth of this assertion and through his own bizarre actions tries to convey this message to others. Clearly his scorn, hatred, and vituperation are directed at the stigma that White racists have placed on Blackness, and he takes it out on Blacks whom he thinks lack his level of education and culture and even his ability to command.

In interviews he has given, Nelson Estupiñán Bass has been consistent in the several comments he has made about *El último río*. He is unequivocal about having set out to have a greed-driven Pastrana cut such a ridiculous figure, and he affirms that all people are equal. That Pastrana continues, even after arriving at that conviction, to exploit Blacks and Whites equally is not out of character, for by that time he has become a tough businessman. Ambiguity sets in, however, when we consider the underlying implications in the novel about racism in Ecuador. Pastrana is a character whom readers should meet, but it would be unfortunate for them to come away from their reading thinking that *El último río* enlightens us only about a negrophobic Negro who exploits his own people. The Black-hating "comedy," as Pastrana himself later calls his "White" period, was play-acting; real White racism is not. This is the more important message that we should take away from this novel, and there should be no ambiguity on this point.

Pastrana makes jackasses out of the White people forced to buy into his fantasy. One such jackass is the police official Cristóbal Vélez, who early on in the novel orders the flogging of this "brawny invincible black man" (*River,* 39). Pastrana emerges from that flogging feeling invincible and capable of standing up to anything. From that moment on he sets out to make fools out of everyone although he gives observers the impression that he is the fool. Cristóbal Vélez is one of Pastrana's first targets; he decides to seduce Vélez's wife. As with Ascensión Lastre in Ortiz's *Juyungo,* Estupiñán Bass intertwined sexual mythology and the issue of race through the encounters of his Black protagonist with White women. Both he and Ortiz capitalize on the sexual attraction between races, and both build into the Black male/White female encounter the element of revenge against and domination of the White race in general. This was Ascensión Lastre's initial motivation to seduce the white María. These motivations eventually disappear in both novels, however, consistent with the maturation of their protagonists, in whom interracial love replaces vengeance. But we should not forget the initial impetus.

"Pretense," "deceit," "fiction," "comedy," and "farce" are some of the words Pastrana himself uses at one time or another to characterize the aberration (to use Estupiñán Bass's word) that Pastrana's "White" period represents, which is why we should not take his crazy actions at that time as more representative than those of his earlier and later periods. Pastrana quickly rises from being a "no-account black man to whom no one paid the slightest attention" to one of the wealthiest and most influential men in the province of Esmeraldas. In Pastrana's experience, four things pave the road to success: talent, tenacity, wealth, and Whiteness. Not being White, Black people have to develop the other three. His own personal goal is to escape the "same old stupid black man" (*River,* 68) label, and the disgust he begins to feel toward other Blacks is leveled at those who allow themselves to be so labeled.

With his celebrated act of lunacy, then, Estupiñán Bass's Black protagonist turns racist rhetoric back on itself, strikes a blow at stigma by dramatically illustrating its negative effects, and demolished two kinds of models that should not be emulated, namely, racist White people and successful Blacks who take advantage of less fortunate members of their own race. All of these things are happening in the novel, which is why readers of *El último río* should not just get mired in Pastrana's negative opinions about other Blacks; rather, they should pay more attention to what drove him to that lunatic frenzy in the first place. Besides, unlike real White racists, Pastrana comes to realize that he has been speaking untruths about Black people. He himself is an obvious contradiction to the perception that Blacks are "brutes who don't even know the letter 'a' " (*River,* 97), which is why he can boast: "I've gotten ahead of all the white folks because of my intelligence and my hard work. Which white has done better than me?" (*River,* 99).

Pastrana's racism, then, is not really his own. His often delirious rant-ings on race reflect racist myths prevalent in the "Fatherland," such as that Blacks are evil, dissipated, shiftless, indulgent, and stupid. His ludi-crous plan to import Whites to crossbreed Blacks out of existence is itself a parody of ethnic lynching or whitening, the practice Abdias do Nascimento once identified as a serious hope in Latin America for solv-ing the race problem.[14] This genocidal idea, like the proposal for steriliz-ing Blacks "para que no den más animales al país"[15] [so that they cannot give more animals to the country] did not originate with Pastrana.

As for Ascensión Lastre, Ortiz's protagonist literally fights battles to disprove those same racist myths. His ambition, like Pastrana's, was to be treated with respect, which he demanded for himself and for all Black people. In *Juyungo* Ascensión dies in a hopeless, suicidal act of bravery trying to steal food from behind enemy lines to save his compatriots from starvation. His daring reads like the action of a man insane, but his *locura* is grounded not in patriotism or class consciousness but in the need to live up to his reputation as a brave Black man who went to war to commit a feat worthy of a Lastre. Despite Ortiz's insistence that class is more important than race, pride in race, whether the author intended it or not, provided Ascensión to the very end with a stabilizing center in his world of struggle, aggression, and injustice. I now believe the same can be said about Estupiñán Bass's character Pastrana, once this contro-versial Black protagonist's *locura* is placed in the proper context.

Chapter Six

Epic, Civic, and Moral Leadership: Manuel Zapata Olivella's *Chambacú, corral de negros; Changó, el gran putas;* and *¡Levántate mulato!*

If slavery and its aftermath do not inform a person's vision of race, that vision is distorted.

William Grier

Manuel Zapata Olivella, the dean of Black Hispanic writers, is making his way into both the Hispanic and Western literary canons. Reading Zapata Olivella's work, we see several Black characters who stand out, including major historical figures—some ancient, some modern—who were leaders in the struggle against slavery and its aftermath. Himself a Black leader, he has written autobiographical accounts of his exploits. He is, as well, part of a distinguished Afro-Colombian family that includes his brother Juan, who is also an author and at one time was a presidential candidate. The recent publication of Yvonne Captain-Hidalgo's comprehensive study in English indicates the increasing interest in the long and productive career of this most prominent member of the Zapata Olivella family.[1]

In her discussion, Captain-Hidalgo examines Zapata Olivella's stylistic habits and thematic constants with emphasis on his aesthetic of the downtrodden. This aspect of his work is what interests me: his focus on heroism and on leaders who overcome entrenched racist perception. One of his singular accomplishments as a Black writer is the example of leadership that both his life and his works represent. His identification with and advocacy on behalf of the have-nots of this world is repeatedly reflected in all of his writing, but the strongest depictions of how obstacles to Black progress are met and challenged are found in *Chambacú, corral de negros*[2] (1963); *Changó, el gran putas*[3] (1983); and *¡Levántate mulato!*[4] (1987). Here Zapata Olivella raises several fundamental concerns of Blacks in the New World, from *Chambacú*'s look at the radical approach to civil disobedience popular in the 1960s to his more recent reflections on Black identity in *¡Levántate mulato!*, both buttressed by and filtered through the epic, Afrocentric view of New World history he displays in *Changó, el gran putas*. Captain-Hidalgo is right to note the paradox of Manuel Zapata Olivella, who "openly proclaims himself to be mulatto, yet [in] several of his works and all of his anthropological treatises project[s] a militantly black self" (Captain-Hidalgo, 165). This militant persona is especially noticeable in these three works. She is also right to note that women are among his leaders. Secondary themes present in these works range from his questioning in *Chambacú*, which was first published in Cuba, of the hypocrisy and interventionist policies of the United States to his interpretation in *Changó* and *¡Levántate mulato!* of the role and phenomenon of *mestizaje* in both his own life and Latin America as a whole.

What makes all three of these books remarkable, however, is their race-specific nature and the extensive compendium of Black exemplars they exhibit. Reading his autobiographical *¡Levántate mulato!*, the reader is taken back to *Changó* and further back to *Chambacú* because, as Nicolás Guillén does in his autobiographical memoirs,[5] Zapata Olivella talks of what these earlier titles represent as well as associated circumstances that stand out in his memory. His other titles, including some theatrical works, are important, as Captain-Hidalgo shows in her study, but these three books stand out.

Zapata Olivella, a Black intellectual, is often the star of his own works, either overtly or covertly through a *persona*, or fictional voice. His uplifting message is embodied in heroic characters whose acts of resistance anchor his aesthetic of the downtrodden. Máximo, the activist protagonist in *Chambacú*, is perhaps the best known of all of Zapata Olivella's creations. More than any other Afro-Hispanic novel, *Chambacú* is a novel of a place, a ghetto in Colombia to which poor Black people were restricted. Zapata Olivella brings this ghetto to life through Máximo, whose heroic example of civic leadership inspires the slum dwellers to revolt against their sorry conditions. The author's task was to create a leader who could cope with tensions in both his family and the community and who would be capable of tapping into the strength of character that Black people harbor and unleashing against those the adversary.

Chambacú has no city services, and Máximo, an intellectual as well as a civil rights activist, wants these fundamental necessities (and the basic right to a decent living) for his people. What they are faced with instead are abuses, forced conscription, and gentrification—their home community is being destroyed to make way for the development of luxury homes for the rich. Zapata Olivella knows Chambacú well, which enriches his narration and makes for the authentic dialogue that is one of the book's strengths. He places us squarely in this world of prostitutes; boxers with colorful nicknames; superstitious medicine men, witch doctors, fortune tellers, and tea leaf readers; corrupt police officials who take bribes and the barkeeps who pay them; and others, most of whom find Máximo a bit strange and view him with suspicion. We are taken inside this Black enclave of 10,000 poor families where one doctor and a lone school teacher fight heroic but often losing battles. In this setting we come to know the story of Máximo; his strong mother, La Cotena; and the disparate family she anchors. Through action and description, other characters come to life: Máximo's not-so-noble brother José Raquel and Inge, his White wife whom he picked up in Sweden on his way back home from the Korean War, where he had served and profited from illegal activities. Though she eventually separates from her husband, Inge chooses to stay in Chambacú to help and becomes, like La Cotena, a civil rights activist under Máximo's influence. We learn a good deal about Máximo from how he interacts with Inge as well as from his relationships with his family and the local authorities.

Chambacú is especially worthy of recognition not only because it pioneered advocacy of civil disobedience as a part of Black protest but also because of its theme of interracial marriage. When this book was written (the 1960s), Black writers in the United States were also producing very aggressive literature. Though *He visto la noche* (1953), the author's firsthand account of developing Black consciousness in the United States in the 1940s, comes earlier, *Chambacú* is the first of Zapata Olivella's works to focus on slum-dwelling Black characters cut off from and contrasted with the well-off Whites who inhabit the upscale parts of town. The spark of resistance was always a part of Zapata Olivella's personality, but I believe his experience in the United States helped shape the aggressive stance he takes in *Chambacú* toward protest and civil disobedience. Now that this work is available in English translation, contemporary readers outside the Hispanic field can discover this powerful novel and witness for themselves a Black Hispanic revolutionary consciousness at work. Máximo, imbued with a determination born of frustration with both the Black plight and those responsible for it, transforms those resigned to being victims into believers while taking on the victimizers. Through rising pride and firm resolve, largely instilled and inspired by the example of Máximo, the people we meet in *Chambacú* are moved to action.

Though Máximo, like Nelson Díaz in Ortiz's *Juyungo,* is an intellectual, he is also, like Ascensión Lastre in the same novel, willing to join the fray at great risk to himself. The sense of outrage that fuels his actions comes as much from a knowledge of Black history as from bearing witness to and living through current affronts. Máximo's rebellious actions initially set him apart from both his family and the community, but more important than what he does is the impact his actions and beliefs have on others. We see the transformation that takes place in several of the characters whose initial reluctance is gradually overcome by the power of his example. By the end of the novel, not just Inge but many others as well have come over to his side, especially his mother, who, in an earlier, desperate act, had burned the books she believed were responsible for Máximo's dangerous and "crazy" ideas.

Máximo starts out misunderstood and alone in his opposition to all oppression, symbolized by the attitude of Captain Quirós. This chief antagonist in the novel, a partner in crime worthy of José Raquel's collaboration, dreams of seeing Chambacú burned to the ground. By opposing first the participation of Black Colombians in the Korean War and later the uprooting of the community, Máximo gives expression to the "crazy" ideas that turned him into a revolutionary leader. Having read history, he understands how the slave past encroaches into the present. Slavery's legacy, however, does not dissuade him from his main goal, which is achieving for Blacks the same right to live a life in dignity that White people have and take for granted. Máximo sought to focus his frustrations in fruitful ways. José Raquel, however, who is ultimately responsible for Máximo's death, worked out his frustrations differently. In a clear case of contrast with the novel's hero, José Raquel is devoid of principle, a slave to pretension, and an example of bad judgment, which he exhibits by turning to the illegal activities he had perfected during wartime. Máximo has other detractors in the novel, and we see them through the multiple contrasts that the author sets up, for example, between Máximo and a mother who hates the influence he had on Atilio, her son who died in the service of Máximo's ideals. Máximo himself pays the ultimate price in his fight against injustice; while leading the protest march that concludes the novel he is killed, shot by his own brother.

Before that, however, Máximo pays for his leadership role by spending time in jail. He is first imprisoned in part one, "Las reclutas" ["The

Recruits"], in retaliation for his opposition to the rounding up of Black youth like cattle to be sent off to war. Though he literally spends time away in jail throughout part two "La botín" ["Booty"], his influence is still felt in the community and even more so when he is released and returns home in part three, "La batalla" ["The Battle"], which continues the war motif on the domestic front. Here Máximo takes up the other major battle, this time against local aggressors who plan the forced displacement of the residents of Chambacú. This plan precipitates the protest march and ultimately Máximo's martyr's death. Resisting a war abroad landed him in prison; waging another at home leads to his death. In both cases Máximo chooses his role. He sees himself as being responsible for raising the consciousness of his people, making them understand why they are poor, and making them realize that they can change their circumstances through their own efforts. He succeeds in these tasks, persuading through actions and words and especially his death. Máximo elevates his leadership role in part three of the novel because he fights not only for Black rights but also against outside control of Chambacú; he is not pacified by the coming of the Peace Corps, which he views as a hypocritical arm of U.S. imperialism. The supreme legacy of this civic leader is that when he falls, others carry on his work.

One interesting aspect of this story is its portrayal of how very different two brothers can be, each propelled by the same circumstances but in entirely different directions. This contrast, perhaps more than anything else in the novel, ennobles Máximo and highlights the steady course for good he was determined to follow. The contrast is apparent, though José Raquel could himself be a compelling character if we look at him not as the shameless person he turns out to be but sympathetically as a war veteran whose wounds left him vulnerable to drugs and drink. There is no glory in this novel for the war in Korea or the Black Colombian troops who participated in it against their will, especially since some of them, like José Raquel, took advantage of the opportunity to make some money illegally. The title of part two of the novel, "La botín," refers not only to the spoils of war but also to Inge, who starts out as José Raquel's "trophy wife" but gradually becomes more than that, as the author uses her to contrast an outside view of Chambacú with how people inside it see themselves.

The contrast between Máximo and José Raquel is paramount, as is the one between Inge and everybody else in the novel. Other contrasts providing tension and insight include those between Manga, the upscale district where poor Blacks go to work for rich Whites, and the Black slum Chambacú; between this isolated Black island community and mainland Cartagena; and between U.S. imposition and local aspiration. As well, contrasts within the Black community itself are described. One of these is generational, with the older La Cotena, her sister Petronila, and Atilio's mother all reluctant to get involved, while Atilio and Medialuna, Máximo's other brother, are among the first to follow Máximo's example.

Zapata Olivella displays a good understanding of how people change under competent leadership, and he is especially convincing in showing the transformation in Inge. When first brought to Chambacú, she was thought to be a prostitute or at best a loose woman, but by refusing José Raquel's suggestion to abandon the town and take up residence in Manga she becomes, like Máximo, a stalwart in the community. In fact, many of the better episodes in the novel revolve around Inge. She not only becomes Máximo's ally in the struggle but a sounding board for his complaints and laments as well. The author uses her as a conduit through which Máximo's case is carried to someone from the outside world. She becomes a sounding board for others. More than anything else, however, Inge is placed there not not just to see the misery through the eyes of someone White but also to experience it. Only by experiencing what motivates Máximo's actions, Zapata Olivella seems to be saying, will White people come to really understand why revolution is necessary.

Chambacú is a talking novel, just as Nicolás Guillén's *Motivos de son* is a collection of talking poems. Máximo leads by example, but he also knows how to shape his words persuasively. Reading this novel is like watching theater. Roberto González Echevarría, as I indicated in an earlier chapter, calls Guillén's *son* poems "mini dramas";[6] Y. Captain-Hidalgo calls Zapata Olivella's novel "dialogic" (Captain-Hidalgo, 165). The talking, however, ranges from staccato delivery to often fiery speeches designed to move masses. Zapata Olivella is focusing on a group of people, but he personalizes Máximo and the others to such an extent that we know them only by their first names. Through Máximo's preachings for Black unity and collective action, messages that Cubena's characters will later carry, and through presenting the individual miseries of these residents, Zapata Olivella creates a very rich novel. He does this not just by means of character development and transformation and stylistic expression but thematically as well. There are many themes in this novel, among them war as a plague, hunger, misery, a mother's pride in family, superstition and other ingrained practices detrimental to Black progress, U.S. intervention, local corruption, oppression, social injustice, interracial marriage, and revolution. *Chambacú* is often considered to be the first Afro-Hispanic novel to call for revolution as a solution to the problems of the downtrodden, but the paradox here is that while on the one hand the novel is antiwar, on the other the author justifies armed rebellion for a good cause.

Máximo is one of the first Black revolutionaries in modern Afro-Hispanic literature, and in this sense he takes his place alongside Agne, the main (fictitious) character in *Changó, el gran putas,* Zapata Olivella's epic accounting of real Black heroes and the leadership they have provided over the centuries in the Americas. From Marco Olivares in an earlier work to Máximo in *Chambacú* and later to Malcolm X in *Changó, el gran putas,* Zapata Olivella is consistent in his presentation of committed Black leaders—both real and imaginary—in a struggle that includes women, as in *Chambacú* with the participation of La Cotena, Inge, and the local school teacher. Agne continues this role but in a much stronger way, in effect, becoming in her commitment a female equivalent of Máximo.

Changó, el gran putas, the product of over 20 years of research, is a much bigger book than all of Zapata Olivella's previous ones, and it is awesome in the historical details that inform it. Whether writing about the Haitian revolution or about the Civil Rights movement in the United States, epic heroes, many of them larger than life, abound. The novel traces the Black story from Africa to the New World and encompasses all of the Americas, but the Black struggle in the United States, especially in this century, and the exploits of the Black leaders that exemplify it take up about a third of the novel. There is something for everybody in search of a Black history lesson. Such familiar names as Nat Turner, Harriet Tubman, Booker T. Washington, Frederick Douglass, Marcus Garvey, Paul Robeson, and of course Martin Luther King and Malcolm X make up the broad spectrum of those who carry forward in successive periods of history not only the expectation that Black people will be free but also that they will have a hand in achieving that freedom. The entire novel moves like a spirit and indeed includes spirits that walk among the living, giving advice so that those living in the present can benefit from the experience and strategies of those who went before.

The novel, expressed in mythological terms, relates the carrying out of the mandate of Shangó, the African god of war who declares that Black people should engage in wars of liberation until all are free.

Though slavery is now a distant memory, Black leaders in *Changó, el gran putas* learn that racism, slavery's lingering legacy, is just as pernicious an opponent. Inspired by such icons as Toussaint L'Ouverture, Black slave masses share the spotlight in this novel and are shown as active participants in their own liberation throughout the Americas. Zapata Olivella shows how Blacks, with the help of ancestral memory and faith in their destiny, were able to keep hope alive. What sustains his novel is the sense of mission that motivates its subjects; the section on Haiti represents the clearest account of the collective faith of a people in their destiny foretold. This "voodoo rebellion" produced Mackandal, certainly one of the most famous maroons, or runaway slaves, in Black history, and other symbols of resistance, Toussaint L'Ouverture among them, whose heroic exploits rival those of the gods themselves. Zapata Olivella presents them as legendary figures befitting the mythical status they deserve. The Afro-Colombian author goes inside the revolt to seek the source of the strength, for example, that made the Haitian revolution—and such earlier rebel strongholds as Palmares in colonial Brazil—possible. He does this by conveying a spiritual and physical unity that withstands all oppressors.

Máximo and other Black heroes in Zapata Olivella's earlier novels are imbued with this same spirit or strength of purpose, as is the author himself. Long before *Chambacú* and *Changó,* Manuel Zapata Olivella had begun to live and write about his own life, doing much of both on the road. The experiences he had in the 1940s in the United States, which he describes in *He visto la noche,* are later incorporated along with other events into *¡Levántate mulato!,* written in the late 1980s. In *Chambacú,* for example, Captain Quiros wants to see Chambacú burned to the ground. This actually happened; the author tells us about it and many other things in this later work. He also describes other incidents and people including his father, perhaps the most influential person in his life. *¡Levántate mulato!,* I believe, is Zapata Olivella's crowning achievement because he is able to weave his own life into the same fabric of history that he writes about in his fiction. As well, he addresses the question of choice in racial identity and what making the the wrong choice means. Zapata Olivella took this discussion beyond duality not just in this work but also in a spate of recent publications that continue to explore his own identity in the context of Colombian and American racial history.

Manuel Zapata Olivella issued his challenge to Blacks everywhere in 1983 with the appearance of *Changó, el gran putas.* In *¡Levántate mulato!,* which he published first in French in 1987 and in Spanish in 1990, he issues another challenge—this time to mulattos to accept their Black identity. In 1974 at the Coloquio de la Negritud y la América Latina in Senegal, Zapata Olivella noticed the apparent lack of public discussion of Native Americans and African Americans together in the same New World context. His position was that we cannot talk about one of these American racial groups without taking into consideration the other, a point he later explored in *Las claves mágicas de América* [*The Magical Keys to America*, 1989]. In this treatise he sets the record straight on the Latin American history of racial mixing by emphasizing that *mestizaje* was the result not of tolerance but of sexual violence during conquest and colonization. Underlying Zapata Olivella's effort is his belief that Black people in America have a responsibility to defend the Native American not only because both peoples are victims of White supremacy and domination but also because they share the same substratum in America's racial mosaic.

Using this as his point of departure, the Afro-Colombian author is adamant that mestizos should accept their indigenous identity just as mulattos should accept their Black identity. What is important here is that he is not talking about theory or a symbolic or philosophical identification but a real one. The height of inauthenticity, in his view, would be to identify in the abstract but without accepting the biological links and the social responsibility of solidarity. To him, identification is more than an intellectual exercise. In his search for Afro-Hispanic identity, he is also searching for what he considers to be an American truth. Manuel Zapata Olivella calls for a radical change in attitude toward race in America.

Identity, to the author of *Changó, el gran putas,* means acceptance, not denial, and this is his message to mulattos and mestizos alike. He had briefly explored this message in *Nuestra voz* [*Our Voice*, 1987], in which he argued how humanly and humanely impossible it would be for mulattos not to identify with Blacks. His belief is that despite racial mixture in America and separation in time and distance from Africa, African influence cannot be erased from the ethnic memory of Blacks. These recent writings are about affirmation, not denial, and in this vein he wrote *¡Levántate mulato!,* to date his most important statement on the Afro-Hispanic identity as well as a personal search for his own identity. One of his purposes in this work is to place Blackness squarely within the traditional context of Latin American *mestizaje;* it is an honest defense of triethnicity and its contribution to the development of a new America. Another is to show that despite racial mixing, the African spirit and presence endure. *¡Levántate mulato!* rescues the terms *mestizo* and *mulatto* from their negative connotations and gives them dignity. Zapata Olivella addresses the Afro-Hispanic identity by considering the mulatto to be the key to that identity in racially mixed Latin America. While he pays homage to his own indigenous, African, and European ancestors, the horrendous nature of slavery moves him closer to Black people. For Zapata Olivella the choice is simple: Either identify with the enslaver or with the enslaved. He accepts this latter identification as a badge of honor, but the Afro-Colombian author does chart the racist pressures that make mulattos want to disassociate themselves from the stigma of slavery's legacy—and from pure Blacks. He clearly understands that the problem of invisibility that Blacks faced in Colombian history led many to believe there was more future in trying to be White if they could get away with it, especially in multiracial Cartagena.

In a sense *¡Levántate mulato!* is a defense of Blackness under siege. By proclaiming his triethnic *mestizaje,* Zapata Olivella addresses the human side of racial mixing. His book is about the moral courage to reject not Blackness but those who would stigmatize it. Let the master be the one to be ashamed, to cite Nicolás Guillén's dictum. Zapata Olivella's White ancestors are tucked away "en algún rincón de mi alma" (*LM,* 257) [in some corner of my soul] but will always carry less importance than the African and the Native American. Other mulattos, in his view, should move away from a Eurocentric image and toward the same catharsis. To do otherwise, in his view, is to engage in a divisive form of "self-ethnocide." Manuel Zapata Olivella puts the best defense of his position in the words of his father: "En cuanto a lo negro, honor tengo en serlo, pues yo no voy a renegar de mis antepasados africanos, traídos aquí como esclavos, ni por ello a renunciar de mi raza, sólo porque usted tenga y considere al negro como un ser despreciable. Y en eso se equivoca, pues cuando la conciencia es pura, el color de azabache no deshonra" (*LM,* 76) [I am honored to be Black. I am not going to deny my African ancestors brought here as slaves. I am not going to renounce my race because of that, just because you might think Blacks are people to be despised. You are mistaken. When your conscience is clear, Blackness does not dishonor]. While he respects the memory of his mother, his father's strong attitude of racial solidarity set the route he was to follow.

Manuel Zapata Olivella did not come by his awareness of his racial identity suddenly. This gradual process intensified once he went to Bogota to study; there he first became aware of the "invisible" racist barriers that, as in Cartagena, kept Blacks and Indians out of the decision-making process. In the big city, he became aware that he, a mulatto, was considered "el negro" [the Black], although in some environments he was light enough to be considered White, and that those barriers applied to him as well despite his qualifications—something that Nicolás Guillén also occasionally experienced. Zapata Olivella also observed with mounting distaste the "brainwashed" Blacks who did not identify with their race. By also taking up the Native American cause, he came to acknowledge ancestral ties and a similar historical exploitation; however, he kept everything in perspective. "Sí, indudablemente éramos negros" (*LM,* 189) [Yes, we undoubtedly were black], he insists but concludes, "Indio, mas siempre negro" (*LM,* 257) [Indian, but always black].

In *¡Levántate mulato!* Zapata Olivella traces contacts between Blacks and Native Americans not only back to colonization but further back to pre-Columbian times, and he points to the Olmecs as one example of that early racial and cultural mixing. He is as adamant about this as he is about the indigenous substratum in the Caribbean, from whence he traces his own Indian ancestors, a view that he further validated during his travels among the poor and dispossessed both in Mexico and in Central America. Ever interested in his indigenous heritage, Zapata Olivella helped establish a Center for Afro-Mexican Studies in Mexico. By the late 1940s, however, his Black identity was so entrenched that he insisted on coming to the United States perhaps to test it and certainly to experience the same trials and tribulations as his Black American brothers.

I consider Zapata Olivella's choice of identity to be a heroic example of leadership because in Latin America, where even Indians are sometimes called Black when insult is intended, being willing to identify oneself as Black or Afro-Hispanic is no small decision. Moral and physical courage are required to do it, but it has to be done. He admonishes mulattos "aún nadaban en complejos raciales" (*LM,* 322) [still drowning in their racial complexes] and Blacks trying hard to infiltrate the ranks of the "mulattocracy" to take that step. Negritude, to him, is a form of heroism in America, rooted as it is in rebellion and hope, two characteristics that have impacted especially on the oppressed majority population in Latin America. His instinct since childhood was toward discovering his origins, long before reading Fanon, Senghor, Césaire, or Damas. His work is an attempt to keep consciousness raising on course and on the front burner of politicians, academics, and others. Like Cubena,

Manuel Zapata Olivella is against racial betrayal, which is what people of color are guilty of doing when they pretend that all is well, aspire to transcend race, and ignore the plight of their less fortunate brethren.

After establishing his Black identity in *¡Levántate mulato!*, Manuel Zapata Olivella moves on in *Las claves mágicas de America*. In this work he shifts attention away from his own personal history to explain and document the historical roots of contemporary America. Understanding that history is the key to understanding not only race, class, and culture in Latin America today but his mulatto challenge and the passion behind his views on racial identity as well. In this work Zapata Olivella outlines in graphic detail the inhumanity of the conquest and colonization perpetrated against Blacks and Native Americans by Europeans. He reiterates his view that racially mixed children were conceived and born but with no love in the process, because *mestizaje* meant sexual violence pure and simple. What was to become a multiracial society in Latin America was not, in short, the result of Christian outreach but rather the lack of available European women.

Zapata Olivella sees no benevolence in the slave history of Latin America, and as proof he points to the eyewitness accounts of such atrocities as mutilation, castration, and burning left, for example, by the Jesuit fathers Alonso de Sandoval and San Pedro Claver. *Mestizaje* as a theory of Whitening and the myth of racial democracy, he insists, are racist theories of denial designed to hide this truth, which is why he considers it important for mestizos and mulattos to remember it. He concludes *Las claves mágicas de America* by pointing out that the new generation is, in fact, beginning to face up to the true meaning of its multiethnic identity by creating new organizations to deal with it. With increased aggressiveness Black, Native American, and racially mixed leaders alike refuse to remain invisible and are changing the attitudes of what he calls Latin American Uncle Toms and brainwashed Native Americans. The key to Afro-Hispanic identity, for Zapata Olivella, is understanding the new American as a triethnic person but one who, for the reasons outlined above and at least in his own personal case, will always be Black.

Thus, Manuel Zapata Olivella rejects the whitewashed version of Spanish colonial history in America. In like manner he rejects the thought that those with a racially mixed background in Latin America should even want to consider themselves White. His objective, however, is not racial hatred but racial enlightenment. Mestizos and mulattos should remember the truth of Latin American racial history so that they will not identify with Whites out of ignorance. Zapata Olivella is a great admirer of W.E.B. DuBois, who once said that "the Mulatto . . . is as typically African as the black man."[7] In Latin America the mulatto, to paraphrase James Weldon Johnson (Johnson, 31–34), is just one of the infinite variations among African people. Considering the current multi-cultural search for roots, Zapata Olivella's reevaluation of *mestizaje* in Latin America could not have come at a better time.

Zapata Olivella leads on the question of choice by taking a moral stance to justify his identification with Black people. Despite his own triethnic background, he understands that given the obstacles and disadvantages they encounter, Blacks need all the help they can get, especially from mulattos like himself, which he is in the Latin American sense. In the first chapter, I talked about the obstacles or handicaps to change in Latin America; these include denial or, as James Brooke puts it, "a low level of racial identification"[8] among Blacks, which has some mixed-race people identifying themselves as something else. This problem is especially acute in Zapata Olivella's Colombia, which has Latin America's second-largest Black population—five million—after Brazil. Some of Brooke's informants tell him that in Colombia today, some Blacks try to be as White as possible. Political consciousness among Blacks is increasing gradually in Colombia, however, fueled by activists who are taking a powerful role in the struggle not just against the low level of racial identification among Blacks but also against the other obstacle or handicap: racism by the nation's European elite.

Manuel Zapata Olivella understands all of this and has always been in the forefront of both of these struggles during his adult life. In *¡Levántate mulato!* he shifts his analysis from his characters to himself, the author, as he tries to define through an accounting of his own life what these obstacles are and how to overcome them. Although other Black role models played a part in Zapata Olivella's life, his father's defiant and rebellious attitude set the tone for his son, and not just because of racial beliefs but also in his other capacities as educator, editor, and liberal thinker in matters of politics, learning, and civic duty. The primary message of *¡Levántate mulato!,* then, is that mulattos have a moral obligation to not turn their backs on Black ancestors who endured slavery by pretending to be White. The defining moment in this work—and in Zapata Olivella's life, I believe—was that time in Bogotá (*LM,* 181) when the author was called "el negro" by Whites (though among Blacks he was taken for White). This moment begs the question his book seems to be raising: why would mulattos want to be White if Whites still see them as Black?

In *¡Levántate mulato!* Zapata Olivella tells mulattos to identify with Blacks because it is the right thing to do. Even his *Changó, el gran putas* highlights some non-Blacks who acted justly. Inge, in *Chambacú,* also sees that the right thing to do is to stay in that Black ghetto to help. By arguing that mulattos have the same obligation, and to an even stronger degree, Manuel Zapata Olivella has assumed a leadership role as much on this issue as he has on others.

Chapter Seven

Black Poetry and the Model Self: Pilar Barrios's *Piel negra* and Gerardo Maloney's *Juega vivo*

Before Manuel Zapata Olivella, there was Pilar Barrios; afterward, there was Gerardo Maloney. Although Maloney falls in the category of Black Central American writer of *antillano* origin that I will discuss in the next chapter, in this chapter I link this Afro-Panamanian poet with Barrios, the earlier Black Uruguayan poet-pillar of his community. Despite being separated in time, these two poets have something in common. Both use their art to express strong concern for and appreciation of Black self-improvement and to point out individuals who have worked to become role models and leaders. All Black Hispanic writers urge Blacks to perfect themselves, the classic example being Guillén's lecture to Sabás in his well-known poem of the same name. In her article "The Special Gift of Literature," Shirley Jackson insists—correctly—that Black Hispanic literature reinforces positive values and self-esteem, making it exceptionally well suited for young readers.[1] Jackson illustrates her point with selections from such writers as Carlos Guillermo Wilson, Quince Duncan, Nicomedes Santa Cruz, and Eulalia Bernard. Stephanie Davis-Lett is right, too, in her contention that Spanish American writers in general and such Black Hispanic authors as Nicolás Guillén and Adalberto Ortiz in particular frequently used the image of Blacks and mulattos to symbolize the national identity either as heroic defender of the homeland or as guardian of the national culture.[2]

In an earlier study I focused on the Black presence in literature in a search for *la especificidad latinoamericana,* that distinctive central or human core in Latin American literature that goes beyond the aesthetic.[3] I saw the presence of Blacks, whether as authors or subjects, as a central element lending authenticity to the concept of humanism in Latin American literature and criticism. My concerns at the time were with critical standards and literary models, specifically the model for literary Americanism that came "from black folk up" (Jackson 1988, 18).

In the search for an authentic American voice, Blacks as forcefully independent, strong cultural heroes often turned up in literature, standing, for example, at the center of the *Afrocriollo* movement. In this first genuinely "American" literary movement of this century in Latin America, the Black as author and as subject represented positive values that transcended the superficial image of the Black as criminal and primitive often found in the literature of that time.

Writing from within their communities, both Pilar Barrios and Gerardo Maloney were able to draw on the example of specific Black individuals who represented not just essential components of New World culture but positive values as well. On a larger scale we can talk about the new American voice, even modern Black heroism as apparent in such works as Adalberto Ortiz's *Juyungo,* in which the conventional White protagonist is replaced with a Black one. Ortiz's macho American from Esmeraldas, who upheld the principles of dignity, justice, brotherhood, and freedom, cannot be ignored in any search for the model self. For years Black writers have been injecting humanist values into the larger Latin American literature, but Barrios and Maloney start at home by making Black people in general and personal acquaintances in particular know that they do matter, that the examples they set are important for themselves and for those who come after. Their message to Black readers is to create model Black selves and emulate those who already have by developing "un plan amplísimo de acción futura" [a bold plan for future action].[4]

Pilar Barrios was the ultimate Black role model, preaching self-improvement in his poetry and in his life. The dean of Black poets in Uruguay, Barrios was a community and cultural leader and a journalist as well, serving as both editor and contributor to the Black journal *Nuestra raza* [*Our Race*] from its inception in 1917 through its later reincarnation in the 1930s and 1940s. The journal, which Barrios used to encourage intellectual growth, fomented social, political, and literary activity and in 1947 even published *Piel negra* [*Black Skin*], a collection of poems that Barrios had been writing since 1917. The journal gave much publicity to outstanding Black role models from around the world and from the community so as to bolster the character and development, both moral and professional, of Black people in Uruguay. Black intellectuals in Uruguay in the 1940s, both men and women, dedicated their professional efforts to combatting the negative social, political, and psychological forces that held Blacks back. They agreed with Pilar Barrios's sister, María Esperanza Barrios, that the press could be a useful weapon in the fight they had to constantly wage on all fronts to improve their lot. Both the cultural and political scenes were battlefields whenever the promulgation of positive Black images was at stake.

The Black press was one weapon, literature was another, and Pilar Barrios used both. Throughout his career, his interest in the Black model self was constant. Barrios's basic messages always were that Blacks should use and develop their intelligence, and much of his poetry is a catalog of those who have done just that—musicians, lawyers, writers, scholars, poets, and soldiers. He preached cultivation of the great human virtues: nobility, idealism, dignity, respect, and morality. Despite rampant negative forces, Barrios was optimistic that one day Blacks would get their due, and he wanted them to be ready. He did not want Blacks in Uruguay to lose hope or to believe themselves inferior, and he rejected as a fallacy the assumption that Blacks were any less than Whites.

In Barrios's time, racism and discrimination did not bode well for the future of Afro-Uruguayans, which is what spurred him to write poetry of encouragement. Other writers, intellectuals, and groups played similar uplifting roles in different ways, but none did so more than Barrios, who took his writing seriously. He was an eternal optimist; he realized that model Black communities are made up of model Black people who above all must think highly of themselves, and he therefore did. Most of all he did not want Blacks to feel crippled by stigma, and his key poem, "La leyenda negra" ["The Black Legend"], shows how difficult this is to overcome. Another key poem, "Raza negra" an ideal statement on the model self, encourages Blacks to keep up the fight against that stigma.

Barrios's audience always seemed to be the youth of his country. He specifically dedicates his poem "Tema racial" ["Racial Theme"] to Black youth, admonishing them to emulate the glorious lives of great Black figures. All of his key poems revolve around the theme of unfair or premature judgment of Blacks. "Tema racial" especially reveals Barrios's obsession with showing that Blacks are capable intellectually and encouraging Black youth to study and prove it. In 1935 he challenged black women "to awaken and bring forth their talents."[5] As a result, in Uruguay today a new generation of writers, including such poets as Cristina Rodríguez Cabral, are doing what Barrios did in the 1940s: using the weapon that literature provides to protest injustice and encourage racial awareness. Their work continues to be important because Blacks in Uruguay are in a constant struggle against benign neglect, unspoken discrimination, indifference, and other hurtful practices that render them faceless. Romero Rodriguez, identified as the head of Mundo Afro, "the most radical of the black groups [in Uruguay]," complained that "seventy-five percent of our women are maids. . . . We get the worst jobs. We live in the most marginal areas. The only reference in textbooks is that blacks came here as slaves."[6]

The increased awareness among Uruguayan Blacks manifests itself in many ways: involvement in the Afro-American religion Candombe and political movements, open confrontation of hostile racial comments, and efforts to change the unspoken discrimination that "has kept a vast proportion of Uruguay's blacks in menial jobs like that of laundry worker, maid, gardener and chauffeur" (Nash, A4). As in Barrios's time, literature and the Black press continue to be important vehicles. *Mundo afro* [*Afro World*], the journal that is the cultural arm of Romero Rodriguez's Black group in Montevideo confronts racism head on while at the same time giving Blacks in Uruguay something of which they can be proud. Closely associated with this journal are some of the new generation of Black poets, who are getting exposure both in a new anthology[7] and in the *Afro-Hispanic Review*.[8] Their work brings a very contemporary message to the racial question in Latin America.

Maloney is part of this contemporary generation. He is already better known than the new Black poets in Uruguay, but his total output matches neither that of Barrios nor that of his Central American colleagues Duncan and Cubena, in quantity. Maloney published *Juega vivo* in 1984. Ian Smart tells us that Maloney's own translation of this title is *Get Hip*, "thereby linking his work with the North American black poetry of the 60's and subsequent periods."[9] Smart's study of this work focuses on some of the formal aspects of Maloney's poetry, but compares, in one instance, the didactic humor of "Cogiéndolo suave" ["Playing It Cool"] to Gwendolyn Brooks's poem "We Real Cool." Thematically, however, Maloney's poem "Amo a mi raza" ["I Love My Race"], which begins

> Amo a mi raza
> porque ha sido odiada
> de siglos en siglos
>
> . . . .
> Amo a mi raza
> negra, fuerte y vigorosa[10]
> [I love my race

> because it has been hated
> for centuries
> . . . .
> I love my race
> black, strong, and vigorous]

is one of the most eloquent statements on behalf of Blacks ever written in Spanish. All of Maloney's poems are consistently positive as he reminds Blacks, as in "Cambios" ["Changes"], of how far they have come and the changes they have undergone since slavery: "Ya somos diferentes / . . . bien diferentes / bien hablados / cultos, / imaginativos, / doctos y preparados, / . . ." (*JV,* 53) ["We are different now / . . . very different / Now we are educated, ready, creative . . ."]

Smart, with good reason, believes Maloney will become one of Central America's most interesting literary figures. Maloney is an intellectual poet, as Smart shows, who sometimes takes a cerebral approach to poetry as did Barrios, but Maloney's intellectualism is never far from or above the use of street humor and word play or other poetic strategies popular in oral literature. Maloney is already recognized as a Black poet who writes poems and uses his creative talents, as did Barrios, to educate and inspire others; in fact, some of Maloney's work falls very much in the tradition of Pilar Barrios's youth-directed poetry of the 1940s. His poetry also recalls Barrios's concern for Black self-improvement in that it is designed to motivate Blacks to take control of their future and history.

In his book on Central American Black writers of West Indian origin, Smart explains how Maloney's poetry is about self-affirmation and pride and identity, about knowing who you are.[11] Smart writes about how Maloney exhorts young people to forge themselves into men and women and focuses on Maloney's fine poem "Nuevos nómadas" ["New Nomads"], but I especially like his poem "Invasión" (*JV,* 85), in which the poet admonishes Blacks to take over not just their little plots of land but history as well. Maloney's poetry covers a good deal of Black history from the first slave ship to today, and it clearly establishes his ties with Africa, the West Indies, and his race. But mainly Maloney is a poet of change and renewal. Such poems as "Líder" ["Leader"], "Cambios," and "Cogiéndolo suave" are among his most significant. These poems (and the title of his book itself) demonstrate an outstanding commitment to the new Black consciousness designed to mold the model self. Playing it cool, for example, gets you nowhere, whereas getting hip does. His message is an inspiring one that encourages all Blacks to join forces for the common goal of developing their potential to the fullest.

Maloney is very conscious of where Blacks came from and where they should be heading, and for this reason he wants each one to examine his or her own life. Perhaps more intensely than any other Black writer in Latin America today, Maloney has his eye on the future; his poetry constantly points to tomorrow. His is a poetry of example, which is why there are so many poems about individual people in his work, real people whose own examples he poeticizes. There are references to such names as "Miss Aines," "Mista Lambert," "Aunt May," "Willy," "Leroy," and "Brayan." In fact, what I like most about Barrios's and Maloney's poems is that they are so full of the names of people who have earned their respect. Maloney's examples, for the most part, are of ordinary people doing an extraordinary job of survival as they go about the business of living, but their examples are no less valid. Maloney sometimes lets them tell their stories as in the poem "Testimonios," where the details of daily living underscore such hardships as hunger, poverty, and deprivation. Converting oneself into a model citizen, however, does not always bring advantage in lives that are often a "lucha día a día" (*JV,* 33) [day-to-day-struggle]. In "Arturo King" the poet chides King Arthur for his misguided priorities. Life is hard enough and becomes even more difficult when enthusiasm for the wrong values drains resources and builds false illusions. In "Willy" as in "Testimonios," Maloney illustrates how the examination in detail of the lives of ordinary people can bring readers closer to his subjects or others who share their reality.

Barrios's names range over history and are sometimes well known; Maloney's could be of a street person, for example, in "Destramp," but one who speaks of the future and whose own state as well as his words recalls the past. Smart discusses the relevance of names in Panama and their importance as badges of identification, especially to Central Americans like Maloney of West Indian descent (Smart 1984, 105–7). The question of names to someone of Anglophone Caribbean background is particularly relevant in view of the special circumstances of their linguistic situation, which, as Smart shows, is related to both the matter of language and the quest for identity. Smart devotes an entire chapter to what he calls this new West Indian literature that writings such as Maloney's represent in Central America. The names of characters in such literature are often the primary indicators of West Indianness, Smart calls it, even though these authors write in Spanish.

Maloney advises Blacks of West Indian origin to make their way with courage, and he admires those who do. Both Pilar Barrios and Gerardo Maloney recognize obstacles but realize that optimism and hope are valuable assets, that a positive self-image is the first step to the creation of the model self. Both want people to get their hopes up and keep them there, which is not an easy task in societies where economies are fragile, work is scarce, and rights are denied. All Black Hispanic writers preach endurance and determination, and Barrios and Maloney are no exceptions. Barrios was a leader in his generation and a pillar of his community. Maloney, in his desire to bring Blacks to the realization that times have changed, is indeed a spokesperson for today's generation of Latin American Black writers.

Chapter Eight

Two Black Central American Novelists of *antillano* Origin: Race, Nationalism, and the Mirror Image in Cubena's *Los nietos de Felicidad Dolores* and Quince Duncan's *Los cuatro espejos*

Me no live Jamaica. . . . Patria mía Panama [my homeland is Panama].
Nenén in Los nietos de Felicidad Dolores

Todos estamos encadenados. . . . Son cadenas de Dios [We are all enchained. . . . They are chains from God].
Ester in Los cuatro espejos

Carlos Guillermo Wilson ("Cubena") and Quince Duncan, like their Central American colleague Gerardo Maloney, should be firmly entrenched in any list of representative Afro-Hispanic authors. Both Cubena, who is currently writing the third volume of his Afro-Panamanian trilogy, and Duncan, the prolific Afro–Costa Rican writer, provide in their novels the breadth of history and the psychological depth that characterize good Black Hispanic writing. All of Cubena's work stresses positive Black role modeling. *Los nietos de Felicidad Dolores* (1991), the second volume of the trilogy, solidifies his leading position in literature of this kind, while Duncan continues to add to the reputation he began to acquire with *Los cuatro espejos* (1973). Duncan believes that *Kimbo* (1990), his latest novel is his best, but I think that *Los cuatro espejos* is most important because it goes to the heart of the identity issue, on both personal and national levels, touching on interracial relationships and the place of Blacks, especially non-Hispanic Blacks of West Indian or *antillano* origin, in Costa Rican society.

Black identity is probably more complicated in Central America than anywhere else in this hemisphere, given the added Afro-Caribbean factors of color, language, and culture. Ian Smart was right when he flagged Central American literature written in Spanish by Black authors of West Indian origin as something new in Hispanic letters.[1] The culture-specific body of work in this genre that has emerged in recent years is indeed unique. Smart is also right to assert that for the Black American, to write is the ultimate act of self-assertion.[2] Cubena and Duncan are assertive Afro-Caribbean writers, each of whom published a novel at the beginning of the 1990s that draws on their own experiences in Central America, but they are very different. Much of what they have to say should be of interest to Black readers throughout the Americas because their works are especially relevant to their concerns.

Perception is important in their works, especially in Duncan's *Kimbo,* as it is in any discussion on race relations today.[3] But what is remarkable about *Kimbo* is Duncan's analysis of how reputation and roots determine who we are and how we are perceived. These factors are important in *Los cuatro espejos,* too, as we shall see, but unlike that work no crisis of Black identity or invisibility takes place in *Kimbo.* However, in a critical courtroom scene, public opinion temporarily puts to the test the Black protagonist's perception of himself. Kimbo stands trial wrongly accused, we later learn, of a political kidnapping for ransom. One premise here, which is the belief that all Blacks look alike, is played out against the backdrop of a parade of witnesses (or narrative voices), some who accuse and others whose faith in his innocence, rooted in lifelong acquaintance with him, cannot be shaken. Once freed he is killed but manages to name his accusers in a letter sent from the beyond (or more plausibly, since he knew he would be killed, written before his death and left behind). Another premise of this novel is the lack of concern displayed for the truth or for Kimbo's fate, even by Blacks paid to lie but who later realize how easily they themselves could be so victimized.

Kimbo is about lies circulated as truth by prestigious, upright citizens who should know better but who are quick to project their prejudices onto the accused even when they are unsure of the truth, especially if the accused happens to be Black. We learn the real truth of Kimbo's character as the novel unfolds; in many ways he is an exemplary person, and he dies trying to clear his name. Since childhood Kimbo has been a role model admired for his positive qualities. We come to know many of them in the novel, which is really Kimbo's life reconstructed through testimony, narration, and his own thoughts. Part of this reconstruction takes us back three generations to Kimbo's grandparents, who were on the first boatload of Blacks from Jamaica to arrive in Limón, Costa Rica. Duncan presents a fine look back to this generation of proud, self-sufficient, tenacious people who, with very little, were able to carve out a living and even make musical instruments on the side from whatever was available. The author explores the importance of roots, family, acquaintances, place, and the value of remembering and emulating courageous examples and deeds from one's own family history. *Kimbo* calls for us to exhibit individual and collective heroism and confront such contemporary evils as racism, sexism, and other manifestations of moral laxity.

Kimbo pulls himself up by his bootstraps but is brought down and killed by forces resentful of his hero status in the Black community. As one narrative voice puts it: "Es que ese muchacho está en la cumbre y es negro y eso les molesta . . . es que ese muchacho es de nosotros, de nuestras entrañas. Ese muchacho somos nosotros"[4] [It's just that that fellow is on top and he is Black and that bothers them . . . it's just that he is one of us, and he is close to us. He is us]. In another sense this novel shows how such outside forces as public opinion affect our destiny, how what one does in life is not as important as how those actions are seen. A touchdown is not a touchdown, to use Duncan's analogy, until and only if the game official says it is a touchdown. Such views go to the heart of identity, because the sum total of one's life should not be surrendered to mere public opinion, especially if that perception represents a betrayal; in other words, Blacks should not feel stigmatized or typecast by someone else's prejudices, and neither should they even care.

From the opening paragraph of this novel, Duncan presents the image of a Black man born to greatness but wrestling against those who would undermine his own once proud concept of self. *Kimbo* shows how determination can be beaten into resignation, but the novel also points to the *samamfo* as a source of strength, a concept he first introduced in *La paz del pueblo* [*The Peace of the People*] and in the short story "Los mitos ancestrales" ["Ancestral Myths"]. *Samamfo,* Duncan says, is a word that expresses "this idea we have at home that the spirits of our ancestors are alive, present all the time there with you."[5] To live in the *samamfo* is to accept that "la vida es un todo que fluye" (*Kimbo,* 126) [Life is one continuous flow] in which the past lives on in the present with no clear division in time. *Kimbo* is built on acceptance of this continuum of existence in the Black mind. The expectation of help and protection from his ancestors—his roots—is part of Duncan's religious view of the world and is central to the novel as are the Anansi tales, or moral stories about survival, that also give direction. These "Anansi the Spider" tales have their origin in Africa but are as popular in Atlantic Costa Rica as they are in Jamaica, and Duncan knows them and their humanized animal figures well. His character Kimbo was nurtured on these stories which, like the *samamfo,* raise consciousness and inspire taking control of one's own life and destiny through positive acts of liberation and affirmation both of self and of others. The letter sent from the beyond—the *samamfo*—to clear his name and restore his positive image among his people thus has a clear precedent in his life.

Duncan's *Los cuatro espejos,* his earlier novel, also takes us inside the head of an achieving Black, Charles McForbes, whose light skin facilitates his entry into White upper-middle-class society in San José but who becomes confused about his place despite his success in the "mainstream world" the capital city represents.[6] Charles becomes part of that world, enjoying the privileges that White people enjoy, but in this novel, which is really about race and how hard it is to escape marginality in the eyes of others, Duncan shows what can happen when someone like Charles begins to believe that race does not matter. *Los cuatro espejos* is timely for readers in the United States familiar with achieving Blacks who believe they have obtained "racelessness" in the public eye. Such people assume, often erroneously, that they are no longer thought of as Black although the stigma of their Blackness—though unspoken or overlooked—remains always on call despite their achievements.

McForbes is married to a White woman, the daughter of a prominent physician. This interracial couple becomes a familiar sight in the elegant social circles of the capital city as Charles tries hard to conform to expectations. Exhibiting luxury to impress others, Charles acquires such possessions as a new car with unnecessary extras that even he feels are excessive, though he was expected to have them as well as a chauffeur. With that level of celebrity comes pressure, and Charles, new to this world, succumbs to it largely because he forgets that he is Black, though others do not. In an earlier study I focused on the journey of self-discovery that Charles, finding himself so far from his origins, makes later on in the novel.[7] What interests me now is the pressure that drives him to take that journey in the first place. The breaking point occurs when Charles becomes locked into a situation where meaning grinds to a halt. Having acquired the "proper" speech, wealth, university degrees, position, and wife, Charles has deceived himself into believing that he has "overcome" his Blackness. Once reality sets in, Charles becomes a "lost person" unable to grasp who he was or is. His problem, as we shall see, is not invisibility but awareness of his unreal, empty existence.

Duncan, logically enough, has Charles speak for the most part in the first person, as if directly into the camera, taking the reader into his confidence. Duncan is very adept at reflecting the musing of a troubled mind searching for explanations. He does this in the first few pages of the novel by describing a kind of out-of-body experience Charles undergoes in a nightmare before waking to an even more troubling discovery, namely, that he had no face or at least could not see one when he looked in the mirror, causing him to think he had gone blind. This nightmare, the beginning of his "breakdown," awakens Charles in the middle of the night, whereupon he observes, "Lejos de mi ser yo veía mi propia mano, quieta, inerme. A pesar de mis esfuerzos, no reaccionaba a mi voluntad"[8] [I saw my own hand, still, motionless, separate from me, not doing what I wanted despite my efforts]. From Charles's dream of feeling foreign to his own body to his waking up faceless the next morning, Duncan sets the stage for his story, which is, in effect, an account of Charles's having lost sight of his true self. Duncan introduces this mirror imagery early on in the novel and repeats it four times—thus the novel's title—until Charles later regains his face the fourth and last time he looks in a mirror.

This frightening chain of events culminates with the realization that he is indeed Black, which he had somehow managed to forget. Charles has married "into society" but for love, which is partly why he is able to internalize his new life so well and to such an extent that when he sees other Blacks, he believes they belong to a race separate from his own. Realizing that he is one of them is immobilizing at first but eventually sets him off on his journey of rediscovery. This realization and his subsequent traumatic awakening comes after attending a lecture on the desperate situation of minorities in Costa Rica, which surprises him, so far removed is he from his own Black experience. The author places significant emphasis on the theatrical existence that characterizes Charles's current lifestyle in the capital city, where role playing and affectation are a norm that Charles also comes to question. His inability to see his face in the mirror dramatizes not only how far he had traveled from his racial roots but also represents his subconscious escape from a reality that had entrapped him into keeping up with his White social level.

However White he feels, Charles cannot avoid experiencing a tinge of Blackness whenever he witnesses other Blacks being abused. Such feelings eventually lead him to experience the inevitable anxiety of a

Black person who wants to believe that color does not matter, certainly his own. José Pastrana, in Nelson Estupiñán Bass's *El último río,* has a similar problem but comes to his senses and stops acting White; so does Charles the moment he feels uncomfortable with his own lifestyle, and he travels back in time and space to discover when and where everything began to go wrong.

Duncan tells the story of Charles's journey to his roots in alternating flashbacks as his protagonist struggles to find some explanation for the current trauma his loss of sight represents. Interwoven with this is his unavoidable empathy with less fortunate Blacks, which increases whenever he personally experiences outright racial hostility rather than the paternalistic acceptance to which he has become accustomed. In such confusing and disturbing moments Charles, like José Pastrana, also hates "a todos los desgraciados condenados negros del mundo, y maldecía, maldecía a todos" (*LCE,* 38) [all the damned, wretched Blacks in the world, and he cursed them all]. Unlike Pastrana, however, who pretends he is White and convinces himself that he has convinced others of this pretense, in *Los cuatro espejos* Duncan's Black character really thinks he is White by virtue of marriage and position and by having adopted so well the values that go with both.

The novel is split, like Charles's life and personality, into two halves that alternate between his previous and more real Black life on the coast that yet he had come to hate and his new but empty White life in the capital city. His new life is so devoid of real substance—and he with it—that no mirror image for him is possible. The unreality of his shallow existence and his complicity with it weighs as heavily on his mind during his current trauma as the life he had left behind on the coast. Charles's face is invisible not because others look right through him as though he does not exist but because *he* no longer can see who he is. Charles eventually faces up to what he has forgotten, that he is a Black man in a White world, and ultimately regains his "sight" in the process.

Duncan has Charles meditate on how Black people in Costa Rica, like Kimbo, are trapped by inescapable stereotypes forced on them by the public mind. The story begins and ends in the present, but in between Charles does return to the coast to again experience the Black world he had abandoned after the death of his first wife. But he returns to his life in the capital city and herein, I believe, lies the main message of Duncan's novel, which is that Charles is the sum total of his experiences. Having light skin and climbing the social ladder into White, upper-middle-class society are not reasons to suppress experiences that have made him what he is, and neither should his Blackness prohibit such ascendancy. What is fascinating about this novel is how the author, through Charles's self-examination, explores how losing touch sometimes happens without plan. What Charles learns is that he could go home again but that he does not have to stay; although he should not hide from himself, he also learns that life moves on and things change.

By the end of the novel, the author has laid bare the totality of Charles's life to both Charles himself and the reader. That Duncan does this in a nonlinear but seamless narrative is a tribute to his skill as a novelist and storyteller. A famous Black celebrity who had "made it" once said, "The ghetto made you want to hide your real identity—from cops, from teachers, and even from yourself. And it forces you to build up false images."[9] Duncan's message is that there is no need to do so. His message for Blacks in Costa Rica (and for the nation as a whole) seems to be that they need not be treated as pariahs. In this regard, his message for Costa Rica is similar to Cubena's for Panama in *Los nietos de Felicidad Dolores*. The two authors, however, do take different approaches on the question of race, Blackness, and nationalism.

Los nietos de Felicidad Dolores is Cubena's Diaspora novel. Though less penetrating psychologically than Duncan's *Kimbo* and *Los cuatro espejos,* it is much broader in narrative and geographical scope. In 1985 Lorna Williams wrote that ethnic particularity and national affiliation are not mutually exclusive terms in Cubena's work.[10] Cubena underscores and builds on this point in *Los nietos de Felicidad Dolores* while enlarging his message. I was privileged to read earlier, partial versions of this work and was thus able to follow the development of Cubena's vision as well as his growth as a writer. As part of this growth, Cubena has always prided himself on his positive treatment of women, not limiting them to stereotypical roles. Important also are Black male role models and the duties they assume in his Afrocentric view of history in general and of Panama in particular.

Cubena's new novel is about Black Panamanians largely of *antillano,* or Anglophone Caribbean, ancestry, but in a larger sense it is a contemporary model for the world because it presents a strong case for ethnic identity at a time when resurgent racism and the backlash against multiculturalism are so widespread. Barbara Solow recently wrote that we study African American history not to assuage White guilt or to engender Black pride but to replace racist myths with a truer understanding of "history."[11] Cubena, however, writes to achieve all three of these goals (and others as well), and his message can benefit all readers. One of the strengths of *Los nietos de Felicidad Dolores* is its unabashed and unapologetic didacticism. *Chombo,* Cubena's first novel, is an indictment of the evils of racial discrimination and prejudice in Panama; the title is a derogatory term applied in Panama to Black Panamanians of *antillano* origin. His second novel, written almost 10 years later, is more interwoven with Black myth and history and is very much addressed to his *chombo* contemporaries—especially to those, like himself, who are living in other parts of the Americas.

Cubena's search, strictly speaking, is not for identity; he knows who he is. He wants a way to bring his message home to others. Though he does not let the system and those responsible for racism off the hook, clearly his primary message now is Black unity, the only way to overcome the "modern curse" inherited from slavery, which is what Frank Snowden, I believe, once called racial prejudice. In fact, the secret word in the novel, *sodinu* (*unidos* [united] spelled backwards), is also the key to Black salvation, a point Cubena makes throughout the novel. In fact, this word was the title of one of the earlier drafts of *Los nietos.* In the final, published version, Cubena places the onus for achieving this unity squarely on the shoulders of "los nietos" of Felicidad Dolores, today's *chombo* generation, the role models for tomorrow.

Cubena underscores this message of unity in many ways in *Los nietos de Felicidad Dolores,* among them by addressing his novel to *chombos* and Hispanicized Blacks alike. He is particularly concerned about antagonisms among *chombos* and chastises U.S. Blacks who show little understanding of Blacks from other cultures. Cubena shows how Black progress and unity have been hindered not only by slavery and racism but also by complicity, betrayal, and conspiracy from within the Black community itself. He is just as hard on African accomplices in the slave trade, for example, as he is on others. He particularly addresses his message to those more interested in carnival and personal achievement than in unity and group success. *Los nietos de Felicidad Dolores* is a novel of descendants, but Cubena, like Duncan, reminds his contemporaries, *los nietos,* of the hard times that *los abuelos* [the grandfathers] of earlier generations had to face. Cubena's main point is that today's *chombos,* who benefited from the efforts and sacrifices of their forebears, should match the generosity of those earlier diggers of the Panama canal, who had so little but gave so much. Cubena populates his novel with successful, professional people, but he credits their success to the care, good training, and education provided under trying circumstances by parents and grandparents, which this generation and future ones must duplicate.

Keeping track of all the characters in this novel is one of the primary challenges to the reader. There are many descendants of Felicidad Dolores—who is no less than Mother Africa, as Elba Birmingham-Pokorny has observed[12]—among them Elsa, Libertad, and Chabela, female characters who play significant roles and carry important messages in the novel. Even negative role models are prominent because they carry the message of how not to be. They include a married couple: Fulona, a hard-drinking, chain-smoking flirt, uninterested in Black history, which she refers to as "esos hombres muertos"[13] [those dead men]; and her womanizing husband Ñato Pataperro, repository of all vices, "mal hijo y peor padre" (*Nietos,* 14) [a bad son and worse father], who is a classic role model in reverse, a bad example for his own children and the next generation. "Basura como Ñato Pataperro hay que eliminar de nuestra familia" (*Nietos,* 187) ["We have to keep garbage like Ñato Pataperro out of our family"], one character states in reference to this unsavory person. At the other extreme Cubena places Guayacarima, a radical Afrocentric student, who initiates a search for his "true identity" and ancestral roots, casting doubts along the way on Western history as taught in schools while claiming the Egyptian pyramids and the title of cradle of civilization for Africa. Between these two extremes are characters trying to live successful lives but who, despite their individual successes, have to come to grips with the humiliating reality of racism wherever they find themselves in the New World. Simon Bolivar Brown, for example, wants to do good works in remote areas but leaves the church and the priesthood for a life as a university professor of Spanish. His decision is made easier by his awareness of the church's historically ambivalent attitude toward Blacks. Hurtful, nightmarish incidents he suffers as a Black aspiring to the priesthood in the United States cement his decision.

In addition to Brown, other Black male role models include Triunfo Guerrero, a university professor; Filhozumbí Williams, a business executive; and Dr. Victoriano Lorenzo Brown, an eminent gynecologist, all *chombo* Panamanians, descendants of West Indians dispersed throughout the hemisphere. Their "scatteration"—to use Ian Smart's term for this diaspora—has taken them to Cuba, Brazil, and the United States, respectively, where they have gone in search of work and a decent living. These educated, successful, and cultured role models are among the group making the trek back home to commemorate a historic event, the transferral of the canal, which their ancestors helped build, to Panama. They are accomplished, proud, and quick to give lessons on Black history to anyone who cares to listen. Litó, whom we know from *Chombo,* reappears as a positive Black male role model in *Los nietos de Felicidad Dolores.* Along with Elsa, Litó commands respect as spokesperson for the author's views.

One of the big differences between the final product and the earlier versions of the novel is the large number of added characters. Having to narrate their stories and genealogies helped make *Los nietos de Felicidad Dolores* Cubena's most complicated narrative undertaking to date. He must have had this direction in mind from the beginning, however, because he called his first draft in 1981 *Afroexiliados [Afroexiles].* The emphasis grew from Black plight to solution, and this change is reflected in the title he gave to the second version, *Sodinu,* in 1983. The change also occasioned a structural shift away from a primary emphasis on "White guilt" symbolized by Bartolomé Ladrón, the dominant character of the earlier drafts, to the *chombos* themselves as a group. In the final version, Ladrón—still consumed with festering hatred for Blacks— is retained but is situated differently in both importance and where his story is interwoven with the larger narrative. Rather than opening the novel and dominating the first 80 pages as before, this slave trader now makes his entrance midway, sandwiched in a kind of flashback between the stories of the *nietos,* having been replaced at the beginning by an extensive scene at the airport where Cubena's characters, all descendants of canal diggers, have gathered for the flight back to Panama.

There are the usual minor changes from one version to the next in names and stylistic preferences, but the larger shift in vision from problem to solution, from the plight of the *abuelos* to the duty of the *nietos,* is what transforms the novel. Cubena especially takes pains to show the continuum of history by linking specific characters to specific ancestors. *Los nietos de Felicidad Dolores* is further enriched by the Afrocentric focus that Cubena gives his narration, which, both mythologically and realistically, moves *chombo* Panamanians from paradise lost to paradise regained through unity. Some of Cubena's history is mythology and novelistic invention, but much of it is not. Felicidad Dolores is his most important, new symbolic invention; she gives final shape (and a new title) to Cubena's novelistic odyssey. Felicidad Dolores is also the repository of all the novel's historical underpinnings, a witness to all the *felicidad* [joy] and *dolor* [pain] that Black people have experienced over time. Her commanding presence serves as a connecting link between Africa and America. As well, she is a prophet in the New World, foretelling both joy and sorrow to come. Inventing this transcending spirit enables

Cubena to combine in his narration specific, personal lineages with the use of myth but in the context of known as well as invented history. Learning from the examples of history is as much Cubena's goal as it is his message. In a way his novel picks up where Manuel Zapata Olivella's *Changó, el gran putas* left off. His work is every bit as ambitious as Zapata Olivella's. *Changó, el gran putas* appeared in 1983, the date Cubena gives to *Sodinu,* the second draft of his novel. As though inspired by Zapata Olivella's epic saga, Cubena went on over the next five years to create his own magnum opus. Zapata Olivella focuses on the rebellious, warrior spirit and the revolutionary effort that Blacks must exert to keep hope alive. Cubena takes up Shangó's challenge and personalizes it in Guacayarima, making him a rebel leader in one of this character's earlier incarnations.

Cubena is a good storyteller who humanizes history by putting a Black face on statistics. As in Guillén's *Motivos de son* and Zapata Olivella's *Chambacú,* there is an oral flavor to Cubena's novel as well, which gives an immediacy to his writing. Throughout we hear people speaking in French, English, Portuguese, and Spanish or in a combination of one or more of these languages. The narrative strategy that this linguistic mixture represents helps fulfill the author's overall design, which is to provide as accurate an image of the multicultural and multilingual nature of the *chombo* presence around the New World as possible. As well, the novel appeals to the senses: it is very noisy and tactile and is filled with Jamaican proverbs, allusions to the aromas of West Indian food, and the sounds of Black-influenced music.

Cubena is an inspired narrator who packs his sentences, which are sometimes a paragraph long, with an abundance of information, much of it reflecting the ironies of history. Often, he combines several words of like meaning into one for effect. Yet his work is accessible despite the lengthy sentences; combined words; abundant languages; complicated lineages; multiple characters, some with body doubles; and the many mysteries, confidences, and secrets to be revealed and exposed. Name symbolism is important, as seen in Libertad Lamento [Liberty Lament], Triunfo Guerrero [Triumph Warrior], and Filhozumbí [Son of Zumbí], but among the many examples Felicidad Dolores clearly is the most prominent. Her name immediately conjures up the pleasure and the pain, the joy and the sorrow that characterize the Black experience. Structurally, a magical transition into the past takes place a third of the way into the novel when, once the group heading back to Panama is airborne, the narration moves back in time, returning to the present for the final third. The novel concludes with an exchange of letters, including an important one from Cubena himself, that brings characters as well as readers up to date. Cubena's letter represents the culmination of his own personal dream and outlines a practical example of his vision in miniature. These literary structures and strategies firmly identify him as a master of his craft.

There is no insoluble identity problem in *Los nietos de Felicidad Dolores* because Cubena has never gotten caught up in the niceties of *mestizaje.* He has a solution, and his novel concludes with his blueprint for it. Cubena builds his vision of Black and especially *chombo* unity on ethnic memory and on living memory as well. Many of his role models are ancient and historical, but just as many of them are contemporary. Cubena insists that *chombo* Panamanians have as big a stake in sovereignty as anyone else and need forfeit neither that right nor the right to be proud of their adopted home and of their contribution to it. Cubena's own experiences are very much a part of his literature. At a recent conference in Missouri, he told those of us in attendance that he writes to keep from going crazy. Such a statement indicates how maddening it is for a writer to try to make sense out of the ironies of history, especially where one's own autobiographical story is involved. Literature is indeed a liberating act of self-affirmation. Cubena may say that he writes to retain his sanity, but I would add that he writes also to retain his identity. Unlike Charles, Duncan's protagonist in *Los cuatro espejos,* Cubena's main characters—at least those who are positive role models—are not troubled by self-doubt. They know who they are and never lose sight of that fact or of their right to be Black, Panamanian, and proud of both. Duncan's Charles McForbes delves into his psyche to figure out where and how he belongs; Cubena's Black characters know they belong, and he incorporates history into the world of *Los nietos de Felicidad Dolores* to help validate this conviction. Cubena does not dwell on Blacks "caught" between two worlds. His single-minded purpose is to support the view that there is only one world; that Blacks have earned a right to be a part of it; and that recognition of the relationship between Blackness and nationalism is good for the mental health of both the individual and the nation.[14] Cubena takes every opportunity to lambast the blatantly racist attempt in the Panamanian constitution of 1941 to deny citizenship to Panamanian-born Blacks of English-speaking West Indian descent. Racial solidarity or unity among Blacks themselves is Cubena's wish, but recognition as Panamanians and respect are equally important, especially because Blacks have contributed so much. Even when Diaspora Blacks return to Panama, which is basically the story in *Los nietos de Felicidad Dolores,* it is with the intention of creating a self-sufficient community.

The kind of self-sufficiency that Cubena proposes in *Los nietos de Felicidad Dolores* could be a harbinger of things to come in Panama if his fears are realized. He is not optimistic about national unity in Panama because in his view this will not happen unless the Black contribution is fully recognized, which he does not foresee. He is especially pessimistic about the future of non-Hispanic Blacks of West Indian descent like himself in Panama once the Canal Zone, their main source of employment, changes hands at noon, December 31, 1999, in accordance with the Carter-Torrijos Treaty obligations. His fear is that once a returning oligarchy following the Bush invasion is in place, the treaty will represent a death blow to *chombo* security (Birmingham-Pokorny, 24). *Los nietos de Felicidad Dolores* is set at that time of this handover. Cubena's characters are in fact returning to Panama to take part in the festivities, but even here he voices reservations about the acceptance of Blacks in the Panamanian national fabric by expressing doubts that the ceremonies celebrating the handing over of the canal will be televised. He believes they will be blacked out so that the many Black descendants of the original diggers surely to be in attendance will not be seen. His implication here is that Panama does not want the world to think of it as a Black country, and it is this kind of racist thinking, he believes, that prevents the emergence of an honest national image. He predicts on one occasion that the treaty will lead to the *chombos'* unemployment, misery, and hunger and thus drive them out of the country, accomplishing at last the deportation that the Panamanian constitution tried to bring about years before in 1941. Cubena symbolizes his pessimism in the final death of Felicidad Dolores, who has survived many reincarnations throughout history until this final death blow to the *chombo* presence (*Nietos,* 204; Birmingham-Pokorny, 24).

In *Los cuatro espejos* Duncan justifies crossing over in integration as long as Black ethnic memory crosses over as well. The self-sufficient community that Cubena envisions in *Los nietos de Felicidad Dolores,* however, is to the Afro-Panamanian author as viable a concept in the national fabric, for example, as a Chinese, Italian, or Jewish community. Though *Los nietos de Felicidad Dolores* is heavily historical, even mythological, the many contemporary stories he interweaves inevitably bring him back to Panama and to the *chombo* experience he knows and tells so well. In fact, the second half of the novel focuses, for the most part, on the contemporary antagonisms they suffer despite being authentically Panamanian. His novel, for the most part, is an assault on all of the obstacles, including Black self-hatred, responsible for marginalizing Blacks in general and *chombos* in particular.

Both Duncan and Cubena adopt the concept of the mirror image. In *Los cuatro espejos* Charles has to face up to his own image, whereas in *Los nietos de Felicidad Dolores* Cubena makes the nation face up to itself and its racism. Though he wants Blacks themselves to first practice the mentality of nationhood but as a viable and economically self-sufficient community within Panama, he does not let the nation at large off the hook and shows, through the creation of some ridiculous characters, how abominably racist views undermine rather than strengthen national unity. Duncan is more optimistic; the white Ester, now Charles's wife, used to hate Blacks.

In Cubena's novel we get the mirror opposites of the families of Juan Moreno and John Brown. Both have the same name linguistically but are miles apart, unnecessarily in Cubena's view, on the matter of race. The Moreno/Brown families best show Cubena's practice of pairing up contrasting people who refuse to acknowledge how much more similar than different they truly are. These two families serve as a metaphor for all the wrong-headed conflict afflicting the country and the Black people in it. Though there are exceptions in both families who point the way to mutual acceptance, Lesbiaquiña, Juan Moreno's oldest daughter, whose exaggerated hatred of all things *chombo* illustrates the enormity of the problem, is the worst of the lot. The Brown and Moreno families are neighbors separated by a room inhabited by Felicidad Dolores, who is responsible for having brought all Africans in the New World together. Foolish divisiveness is summed up by Juan Moreno himself when he says such things as "Me llamo Juan Moreno. Negro, pero no chombo" (*Nietos,* 120) ["My name is John Brown. I'm black, but I'm not a *chombo*"] or "Somos negros, pero gracias a Dios no somos chombos" (*Nietos,* 132) ["We're black, but thank God we're not *chombos*"]. Cubena depicts the mirror image motif in a concrete way in the first face-to-face meeting of John Brown and Juan Moreno; both men run away "como quien se espanta de su propia sombra" (*Nietos,* 120) [like someone who is afraid of his own shadow].

In his portrayal of the reluctance of Hispanic Blacks to acknowledge racial kinship with *chombo* Blacks, Cubena carries the mirror image motif to a hilarious extreme. Duncan, in *Los cuatro espejos,* has Charles look in a real mirror to discover his own Black self-hate; Cubena has his Black characters look at other Blacks with hatred because what they see reminds them of what they do not like in themselves. As well, this exaggerated hatred also suggests that acceptance in Panama even of Hispanic Blacks is so fragile that they do not want to be lumped in with the newcomers who arrived in this century to help build the canal. The *chombos* accepted Panama but were never made to feel that Panama accepted them, especially because their language background (English), religion (Protestant), and culture (West Indian) were so different.

The mirror, then, reflects one's soul in Duncan's novel and one's flip side in Cubena's. Cubena also uses the mirror to hold up society's imperfections for all to see. In chapter 5 I said that Pastrana's rantings and ravings on race in Nelson Estupiñán Bass's *El último río* have to be looked at in part as a mirror held up by the author to reflect white Racist thought back onto its source. The same thing happens in Cubena's *Los nietos de Felicidad Dolores,* especially in the character of Lesbiaquiña. As Birmingham-Pokorny points out, Lesbiaquiña is a "perfect embodiment of a large sector of the population of Panama and Latin America that still refuses to see his/her image in the mirror, and is frightened by the possibility of seeing himself/herself reflected in the face of the other" (Birmingham-Pokorny 1993, 148). Lesbiaquiña is the kind of person that Charles McForbes would have become had he not, like Pastraña, come to his senses. Duncan holds a mirror up to Blacks so that they can see what they have become or are becoming. Cubena holds a mirror up to society so that both white racists and Blacks who want to be White can see themselves as the ridiculous figures they are.

Cubena is blatant and to the point. The four mirrors in the title of Duncan's novel, however, represent a gradual, four-stage process of recovery that the author charts through Charles's periodic looks in the mirror, slowly seeing his face take shape as he comes to terms with his real identity. The basic premises of both novels, though, are identical: Blacks have a right to space in the national fabric and not just on the margins, and Blacks should not forget where they came from or change from what they are. As well, both novels link Blackness to nationalism, demonstrating that it is healthier both individually and collectively when people unconditionally accept themselves and others. A healthy absence of pretense provides the remedy for resolving racial ills in Zapata Olivella's *¡Levántate mulato!* Dropping all pretense is also the key to progress in Estupiñán Bass's *El último río.* The novels of Cubena and Duncan, like these of their colleagues, are also concerned not just with how other people see Blacks but with how Black people see themselves.

While Blacks and non-Blacks alike have much to learn from *Los cuatro espejos*, Duncan's novel shores up the individual Black, assaulted by guilt, unsettled by doubt and assailed by conscience. He seems to suggest that suppression of self is as bad as oppression by others; Black people should feel comfortable with success and citizenship and have the right to enjoy them without amnesia and denial. Unlike Cubena's novel, which is blatantly Afrocentric, Duncan's is integrationist, which is why Ester's statement about chains quoted at the outset of this chapter is important: Those chains represent the ties that bind regardless of one's past. This motif argues, as strongly as any other, against the kind of marginalization that Blacks, especially those of West Indian descent, experience in Latin America. Duncan also raises this same argument when he has a policeman say to Charles in San José: "Aquí no estás en Limón: Cuídate" (*LCE,* 120) [You're not in Limón here. Be careful] and when he has one of Charles's friends make the following complaint: "Mirá, en Argentina soy gringo o brasileiro. En Perú soy de Lima, o de la costa en todo caso. En Chile soy gringo o brasileño. En Nicaragua de Bluefields. Carajo y me hablan en inglés o en portugués, nunca en español" (*LCE,* 117) [Look, in Argentina I'm a gringo or a Brazilian. In Peru I'm from Lima or, in any event, from the coast. In Chile I'm a gringo or Brazilian. In Nicaragua I have to be from Bluefields. Dammit and they speak to me in English or in Portuguese, never in Spanish].

Taken together, to read Duncan's *Los cuatro espejos* and Cubena's *Los nietos de Felicidad Dolores* is to experience the double obstacle of marginality and denial, both internal and external, created by racism in Central America.

Chapter Nine

Dominican Blackness: Blas Jiménez's *Caribe africano en despertar* and Norberto James's *Sobre la marcha*

> This is your country. You have to fight for this country. Don't think about anything else. *This* is your country.
>
> Norberto James's grandfather

> You're not a Dominican. Take a look at our two last names: James Rawlings. Besides, I don't want them to call you *cocolo*.[1]
>
> Norberto James's grandmother

The contradictory quotations above point to the unresolved conflict confronting Black identity in the Dominican Republic. The issue of race, Blackness, and nationalism is as problematic there as in Panama and Costa Rica. Thus, this chapter can be read as a continuation of the previous one. Even though the Black element plays as much a role on this Hispanic island as it does in Central America, the phrase "Dominican Blackness" is a contradiction in terms to many. Some Dominicans refuse to speak about the race question as it applies to their country.[2] This fact alone makes the works of Blas Jiménez and Norberto James worth reading, because they show no such reluctance. For them, the term *Dominican Blackness* is another way of saying *nationalism*, and this is true both for Hispanic Blacks and for Black Dominicans of English West Indian ancestry who write in Spanish. For most others, however, the Haitians are the Blacks on the island of Hispaniola (James, 59). In fact, as a result of sharing the island with Haiti, nationalism in the Dominican Republic often simply means accentuating ethnic and economic contrast with its Black neighbor.[3] This contrast is carried to an absurd extreme when Dominican Blacks are referred to as "dark Indians."

Though the Dominican passport division has officially started to designate Blacks as *trigueño*, "dark-complexioned" (James, 59), the fact that this change was so long in coming is indicative of where race relations stand in the Dominican Republic. Norberto James once said that Dominicans do not want to talk about race because "to speak of it would be to discover that we are all black" (James, 58). He sees no reason to stick the label of "Indian" on Black Dominicans, and both he and Blas Jiménez reject it. James believes the label is used in Santo Domingo "para no decirte 'negro' porque creen que ponerte 'negro' en un documento es ofenderte"[4] [in order to not say "black" to you because they believe to put that name on you in a document is to offend you]. James is not offended to be called Black: "Yo me negué rotundamente a que me pusieran 'indio oscuro' porque no soy indio, yo soy negro—un negro de carajo" (Davis 1987, 18) [I flatly refused to let them call me "dark Indian" because I am not an Indian, I am a Black dammit]. Jiménez is even less charitable about the use of this label, considering it a racist attempt to render Dominican Blacks officially invisible; as he writes in "Indio claro"[5] ["Light-skinned Black"], some people resist Black Dominicans calling themselves Black because if they do, that would mean others would have to admit that they, too, are Black. These stances underscore the pride in their Blackness that these two writers have in common as well as the different ways of expressing it that sets them apart.

My interest here in these two poets is heightened as much by their differences as by their similarities. Both are proud Black Dominicans, and they let the reader know it; however, in his poetry Jiménez's Blackness is blatantly expressed, whereas James rarely if ever uses the word *Black* to make his points. Blackness is inherent in James's work but negritude, he once said, is not programmed into it (Davis 1987, 17). Both James and Jiménez are among the newest Black Hispanic writers to attract interest in the United States, where James now lives and where both are frequent participants in symposia and discussions on Afro-Hispanism in general and on the Dominican Republic in particular. They are sought after because their works are current, accessible, and carefully crafted for their audience, which they address directly. As well, they are articulate in both English and Spanish. What I like most about Jiménez's *Caribe africano en despertar*[6] (1984) and James's *Sobre la marcha*[7] (1969) in particular is that both books are positive statements about identity and the Black presence in a country where color, though recognizable, is not always recognized. The phrases *en despertar* [awakening] in one title and *sobre la marcha* [on the move] in the other both convey from the outset this positive spirit. Like their other works, both of these collections counsel Blacks on how to make the best of a bad situation, and both make claims on nationalism. The word *africano* [African] in the title of Jiménez's book also points to the identity question, and numerous poems in this collection and his other works address it as well.

Jiménez strikes a major blow against invisibility by asking searching questions about Black and national identity. He does not hesitate to proclaim his own Black identity, and takes as his mission the task of forcing others to do the same. His primary objective is to upgrade not only Black identity but the image of the Black-as-Dominican as well. Like Manuel Zapata Olivella, Blas Jiménez takes a stand against the erosion of Black identity. Just as the Afro-Colombian author does not wish to be subsumed under the rubric of mulatto, his Afro-Dominican colleague also rejects the official label of *indio*. Jiménez's poem "Tengo" ["I Have"] recalls Guillén's laudatory composition of the same name but unlike the latter's better-known poem that gives praise to the Cuban revolution, Jiménez's version is much more Black-based. "Tengo que sentirme negro"[8] [I have to feel Black], he writes, because that is his obligation and the first step to identity. Like Zapata Olivella, Jiménez rejects the idea of Latin America as being White, arguing that the Dominican Republic is as much Black as anything else. Like Cubena, Jiménez decries pretense and deception, especially self-deception by those who would not acknowledge this fact. Dominicans, he says, must define themselves realistically and not be reluctant to work at that definition. Throughout his poetry he condemns Blacks who wish to be White but also highlights the light-skinned person who identifies with, accepts, and willingly chooses to be Black.

Both Jiménez and James in the Dominican Republic, like Cubena and Duncan in Central America, are very proud of their identity and speak of inherited pride in their works. Charles McForbes, Duncan's Costa Rican character, does this in *Los cuatro espejos* when he talks of his "orgullo jamaicano" [Jamaican pride], and so does Jiménez when he refers to his *orgullo de cimarrón* [rebel pride], the legacy of his grandfather, to whom he dedicates *Caribe africano en despertar*. Jiménez tries to transfer this same pride to his readers by admonishing them to transform themselves "por dentro" (*Caribe*, 54) [from within]. He considers this transformation a necessary first step toward acquiring the strength to break free from imposed molds and expectations. If Black people are to help create a new and fairer history, then a revolution, he believes, has to come from within. Repeatedly in *Caribe africano en despertar*, Jimenéz's poems echo the following well-known words (which lead off the second part of his book) of Aimé Césaire: "Debido a una inesperada y saludable revolución interior, ahora rindo honor a mi fealdad repugnante" (*Caribe,* 37) [Due to an unexpected and healthy internal revolution, I now pay homage to my repugnant ugliness]. Jiménez writes popular and accessible poetry, but writing for him is a mission because he understands the potential that words have to change the present and shape the future. Neither Jiménez nor James is overly political in their works, though there are references that show who their political heroes are and are not.

James's poetry is especially quiet on all of the issues it raises but is in its subtlety no less powerful, uplifting, and encouraging than that of Jiménez. Many of Jiménez's poems, on the other hand remind me of works by other Black Hispanic poets that go straight to the heart of the Black experience. Some of Jiménez's poems do for the Dominican Republic what his older colleagues' writings have done for their countries, which is to force Blackness into public consciousness. In this sense, Jiménez recalls the work of Guillén and Artel; James does not. Rather, reading James's poetry is like reading the work of Pablo Neruda or César Vallejo, though the subject matter is entirely different. James has not written much, but "Sobre la marcha" and other poems included in *Hago constar* [*I Make It Known*], including "La provincia sublevada" ["The Rebel Province," 1972], are worth reading. In addition to the positive message they carry for Black people, his poems are sustained with words associated with César Vallejo such as *angustia* [anguish], *tristeza* [sadness], and *dolor* [grief], but here they are applied to a different experience in the world. The "dolor constante / —casi desdoblándonos" (*Marcha,* 19) [constant pain / —almost turning us inside out] that will reign until "dignidad" (*Marcha,* 21) [dignity] is restored to one and all is cosmic, metaphysical, and universal but expresses a very specific political experience and racial awakening as well. Grounded in the 1960s, when he and his generation came of age, James tells us that the verses of *Sobre la marcha* were inspired by the military occupation of the Dominican Republic in 1965, when the use of violence was put into practice as a main instrument of the government (James, 52). Much of his work bears witness to the events of that time at which he was forced, once he began writing, to take stock of himself and to define his identity.

Norberto James is admittedly an admirer of Vallejo and Neruda (Davis 1987, 19), and like them he speaks through his poetry for others as well as for himself. He even leads off his volume of poetry with a well-known quotation from Pablo Neruda in which the Chilean poet states his intention to write for all people, even for the unlettered who cannot read it. This sentiment is shared by other Afro-Hispanic poets today,

Blas Jiménez and Venezuela's Antonio Acosta Márquez among them, but James also writes in the same free-verse, conversational style that engages the reader in an implicit dialogue with the poet. James's poetry reflects the anguish we see in Vallejo's poetry, but he also focuses on belonging and on rejecting stigma. Unlike in Cubena's works, anger in James's poetry is muted. Yet he is just as firm in claiming for his people a right to space—and a right to occupy that space with the same tranquillity that everybody else takes for granted.

"Sobre la marcha" is the first and longest poem in the collection that carries its name. Because of the kind of encouragement it conveys to those who must transcend pain and learn from experience, this poem represents the kind of fresh material that Shirley Jackson correctly believes today's students need to read.[9] "Sobre la marcha" is about overcoming obstacles and not giving up. What people, especially young people, learn from this poem is that even mistakes, which are part of growing up, teach if we learn from them; that to be on the move is the only way to experience all the emotions that life has to offer; and that life itself is a learning experience and not always pleasant, but one must work through the pain. Learning from mistakes and growing from experience are facets of human existence that transcend race and are good for everybody but are especially applicable to those who must confront, through no fault of their own, more than their share of roadblocks and must do so without losing hope. James's poetry is filled with encouragement because the poet outlaws defeatism and resignation. In his poetry ambition and hope override and conquer anguish, sadness, tears, grief and obstacles. "Sobre la marcha," in short, is a poem about living fully the life that we make for ourselves and fulfilling our dreams despite setbacks. It is an upbeat poem that promises light at the end of the tunnel for people who stay the course.

James's own life provides an example for us all. Born into poverty on a sugarcane plantation, he set education as his goal. He learned Spanish at the age of 10 and later, steeped in the poetry of Vallejo and Neruda, taught himself how to write in their language. He eventually earned university degrees and is now a university professor as well as a poet.[10] Following an active period of writing political protest literature in the 1960s, most of which is now lost, James settled down and started to write literature with a capital L, as he puts it (Davis 1987, 16). Fashioning his experiences into artistic expression, James wrote *Sobre la marcha,* his first effort to take seriously the business of writing, although he also wants us to know that in this volume, "hay de la política y problemas sociales" (Davis 1987, 17) [there is something on politics and social problems]. While they are not blatantly expressed, this volume does address social, political and national problems that reflect his association with leftists as a student in the 1960s and 1970s.

James is proud of his achievements in education and poetry, and he tries to instill in others the same program for success that he set for himself. For this reason "Sobre la marcha" is a tremendous confidence builder. In this work the poet gives strength to his audience by virtue of his own identification with them. From the opening stanzas, which contain the verses, "En cada caída que acontece / hay un imperceptible pero seguro ascenso" (*Marcha,* 11) [In each setback that happens / there is forward movement, however imperceptible], to his reassuring and now well-known concluding words, "Yo no soy un extranjero más. / Soy sencillamente uno de ustedes . . ." (*Marcha,* 26) [I am not one more foreigner. / I, simply put, am one of you . . .], James convincingly erases the distance between his own experiences and those of the subjects of his poetry. This identification is also especially strong in the poem "Los inmigrantes" (*Marcha,* 45 – 49) ["The Immigrants"].

In 1969 James won a prize for "Los inmigrantes" in one of the most important literary contests of that time (James, 54) from the Autonomous University of Santo Domingo. With the publication of this poem that same year in *Sobre la marcha,* James introduced, as Pedro Conde Sturia writes on the back cover of *Hago constar,* the epic story of *cocolo* immigrants as a theme in Dominican literature. James wrote "Los inmigrantes" in homage to his forbears: "As a third generation 'cocolo,' I lived through and freed myself from the economic and intellectual slavery that my parents experienced and experience to this day. . . . I felt the moment had come to reclaim for myself and for them the place which we had earned for ourselves as a part of the Dominican people" (James, 54). James credits this poem with bringing about a better appreciation of the *cocolo* community in his country.

"Los inmigrantes" is a work in progress or at best a shorter and unfinished version of what James originally had intended it to be. A casual reading of this poem reveals many names of people he honors; his original intention—and his ultimate goal, still unrealized—was to devote a poem to each of these individuals. Partly for this reason, the poet assumes the voice of respectful spokesperson whose own present experiences are part of the unfolding history of people who are his subject and to whom he pays tribute. When the poet writes of their earned right to respect and to a place in the nation, he again counts himself as one of them as he did in "Sobre la marcha." He comes to them, as he says, to write their names and their story that "aun no se ha escrito" (*Marcha*, 45) [is not yet written]. Just as Cubena does for the *chombo* in Panama, James accords dignity to the *cocolo* in the Dominican Republic by turning a derogatory term into a badge of honor. Both in this poem and in published conversation, James reclaims for himself and for them "the place which we had earned for ourselves as a part of the Dominican people" (James, 54).

In "Los inmigrantes," James calls for the incorporation of *cocolo* immigrants and their descendants into the national life of the country. He admires those who, like himself, are aware of the negative connotation of the term *cocolo* but who do not allow themselves to feel less Dominican because of it. What is remarkable about James is that while he knows who he is, a Black *cocolo* fully aware of his background and of the racist history of his country, he seems convinced of his total integration into Dominican society, so much so that when he writes, he does not allow himself to think in terms of color or race. He writes, he says, simply as a Dominican author (Davis 1987, 17) and not as a Black. He wants to bring others into that same consciousness because he knows that others of his generation are not as confident. Nicolás Guillén wanted to make the *Afro* in *Afro-Cuban* redundant; James is trying to do the same thing with the *Afro* in *Afro-Dominican*.

By thinking of himself simply as a Dominican who writes, James manages to allow the race issue to flow naturally without calling too much attention to itself. James states his case quietly and within the context of belonging rather than exclusion, and he insists on taking this belonging for granted, especially in light of the sacrifices that his ancestors had to endure to make his acceptance possible. The Chilean poet Neruda once said that readers can find out who he is by reading his poems. Examining James's poetry tells us a great deal about who this Dominican poet is or at least about what is on his mind. This is especially true in such poems as "Los inmigrantes." When James writes, "Vengo a escribir vuestros nombres" (*Marcha*, 47) [I come to write your names], it is easy to consider this poem as his version of *Alturas de Macchu Picchu* [*The Heights of Macchu Picchu*] in that, like Neruda's celebrated signature piece, James's poem gives voice to the long deceased. And like Gulllén's "El apellido," the poem speaks to a present-day audience of third-generation *cocolos* but through it to those earlier generations that provided inspiration. Clearly the *cocolo* is James's inspiration in this poem even though he says he was not thinking in terms of race or color when he wrote it.

James does not address the Black problem in the Dominican Republic but rather Dominicans who no longer should think of themselves or be thought of as Black in an exclusionary sense. In "Los inmigrantes" James writes a success story, his own included. When he says in the conclusion that he is not a foreigner but rather "one of you," he means he is *cocolo* but also Dominican. Transcending the negative connotations of *cocolo* does not mean that Black Dominicans should abandon it; instead, they should wear it proudly. James does not deny that a racial problem exists in the Dominican Republic but he understands why Dominican writers do not like to focus on it. Thus, he does not dwell on the race issue like his colleagues, but he is unique among them in that race does inform his poetry.

James certainly is more idealistic than Blas Jiménez. He likes to believe that to the average Dominican, color does not matter, which is why he gives the benefit of the doubt to those who would stamp "Indian" on his passport. Just as we can read César Vallejo for the "Indian" or mestizo experience or Pablo Neruda for the White Latin American experience, we can read James's work for the negritude experience. In all three cases, a blatant statement on race will not be found, but we do come to know who or what these poets are through their writings. James tries to rise above race to write of other problems that threaten national pride and the stability of the nation. Race as a subtext, however, is unavoidable in a multiracial country. For this reason Black literature by James and Jiménez and by other Black writers in the Dominican Republic is a topic of increasing interest to Afro-Hispanists.[11] The same can be said about Black Hispanic literature in Latin America in general.

Chapter Ten

Passing the Torch: Nicomedes Santa Cruz's *Ritmos negros del Perú* and Antonio Acosta Márquez's *Yo pienso aquí donde . . . estoy*

I don't think we can forget, for the time being, the traditional forms. They are the ones the people know.

Nicolás Guillén

When Nicomedes Santa Cruz died in 1994, one of my students, a Peruvian studying in Canada who knew him, was deeply saddened by his passing. As a moving homage to his compatriot, this student prepared an oral report that included song and recitation, which was both fitting and appropriate because Santa Cruz was known foremost as an oral poet who often sang and recited his poetry on radio, recordings, and on stage. No poet in Latin America reminds me more of this Afro-Peruvian *decimista* than Antonio Acosta Márquez, the Afro-Venezuelan popular poet whose first book of poems was later published in an enlarged second edition.[1] Both of these poets fit into a tradition inhabited by predecessors such as Nicolás Guillén, greatly admired by Santa Cruz, and Candelario Obeso, whose *Cantos populares de mi tierra* is often cited as a nineteenth-century forerunner of modern Black poetry. Nelson Estupiñán Bass— despite his novels, some of which are experimental in form, and his erudite poetry—also belongs in this tradition for his books of poetry written in popular verse form.

Estupiñán Bass created in two separate volumes outspoken black *payadores,* or poet-singers, in *Timarán y Cuabú* (1956) and later in *El desempate* [*Breaking the Tie,* 1978]. Both volumes, good examples of popular folk forms adapted to written literature, use the desafío (or *contrapunteo* or *argumento* as it is alternately known), a poetic mechanism for airing contrasting views through improvised responses.[2] Estupiñán Bass is in good company in Ecuador because his recreation of the *desafío,* as

Laura Hidalgo Alzamora has shown is, along with the *décima,* a representative Black oral art form in the province of Esmeraldas.[3] Alzamora is one of many researchers who have collected examples of work by authentic living *decimeros* in that country. Juan García Salazar, another of these researchers, believes oral literature, especially the *décima,* is quite abundant in Ecuador, judging by the number of Black Ecuadorian poets who engage in *argumentos,* the poetic duels that often take shape in *décima* form.[4] Salazar believes that like written literature, radio can play an important role in preserving and disseminating this tradition.

Estupiñán Bass, Guillén, and even Obeso have left works in other genres, but Santa Cruz and Acosta Márquez were more dedicated to popular verse than to any other form, and both show pride in being able to touch people in ways most likely familiar to them. Both have done their part to pass the torch, which Black Hispanic poets have been doing for years, even centuries. Keeping tradition alive from one generation to the next is especially evident in popular poetry, particularly when it makes the jump from oral or folk to written or formal literature. Obeso, Guillén, Estupiñán Bass, Santa Cruz, and Acosta Márquez have been instrumental in this regard; whether their work takes the form of *son, décima,* or *copla,* all of them hearken back in their own way to that era before authored literature became a vehicle—and even after, if we include the anonymous poetry "whose authorship is claimed by none"[5] that still exists today, for example, Afro-Cuban oral poetry from the Yoruba, Bantu, and Náñigo cultures. The anonymous oral literature of folk tales, proverbs, and songs, and the popular work of such eighteenth-century improvisational poets as José Vasconcelos ("El Negrito Poeta") in Mexico and Meso Mónica ("El Negrito Dominicano") in the Dominican Republic helped set in motion the tradition that later black poet-singers were to make their own.[6] Younger Black Hispanic authors today continue to build on what their predecessors started, raising the issue of justice in their work and passing on the boldness they themselves inherited to those coming after. Whether continuing the oral tradition, raising popular verse to the level of "fine art," or writing poems that because of their authenticity are destined to return to the people who inspired them, each one participates in this tradition.

Nicomedes Santa Cruz did not even admit to any difference between popular and erudite poetry; he demanded the same respect that the cultured elite of his country gave to others (and that Guillén clearly got in Cuba). In his recent book on Guillén, Ian Smart respects the Afro-Cuban poet as much for what he has in common with the reggae music of The Mighty Sparrow and Bob Marley as for anything else he has done. For this reason he approaches Guillén's poetry with "the Caribbean reader/listener" in mind.[7] Smart also recognizes one of the points that Laurence Prescott makes in his recent book on Candelario Obeso: judging by the meter and verse forms employed in his poetry, the nineteenth-century Afro-Colombian poet was deeply familiar with the popular oral poetry of the region.[8] As well, Smart correctly sees some linkage between Guillén's and Obeso's oral poetic forms and Santa Cruz's *décimas,* which, in his view, supported by Henry Richards and Teresa Cajiao Salas's recent finding,[9] represents the culmination of the creative evolution from orality to the written form in Peru.

That Guillén had a hand in this evolution is no surprise, which is why Antonio Acosta Márquez would later dedicate the title poem of *Yo pienso aquí donde . . . estoy* not just to all the people of his race but to Nicolás Guillén in particular. This trail of linkages through Guillén leads from Nicomedes Santa Cruz to Antonio Acosta Márquez and beyond, but whereas Acosta Márquez has no academic aspirations for his poetry, Santa Cruz is a performance-oriented poet who is serious about his work, pointing out that Blacks do not improvise *décimas* in Peru for diversion only. Using himself as an example, he reminds readers of the negritude he injected into his verse beginning in 1955, claiming with pride in the introduction to *Décimas,* a 1971 edition of his works, to be the first Black writer in Peru to write about social problems.[10] Just as Guillén did in *Motivos de son* and Acosta Márquez was to do in *Yo pienso aquí donde . . . estoy,* Santa Cruz in *Ritmos negros del Perú* captured black life in his poetry while trying, at the same time, to preserve the *décima* tradition. In fact, he proudly tells us in "Al compás del socabón" (*en socabón* means "sung to guitar accompaniment") that this is indeed his mission (*Décimas,* 261).

Ritmos negros del Perú, the expressive title of another edition more easily available (published by Losada), was edited by Jorge Lafforgue and also contains *décimas* and other poems taken for the most part from the poet's previous works.[11] This volume, published in Buenos Aires, brought the poet to a wider audience outside Peru, where he was already known for his work on radio. Just as Black rhythms coalesce into the *décima,* Santa Cruz's knowledge of Black history in Peru does the same. But Santa Cruz does more than just preserve tradition; he uses it to teach and preserve Black history itself, especially slave history. When Jorge Lafforgue put together this edition, he admonished the reader to *hear* these poems because he knew they were written for the ear. Reading poems, he suggests, is but one way—and not the best—to appreciate Santa Cruz's poetry. Another way is to hear the poet recite and sing, for example, on *Cumanana,* a boxed set of records from 1964 of Santa Cruz in performance, and I count myself among the lucky ones to own it. *Ritmos negros del Perú* was, in fact, undertaken in response to public demand, for works made popular through his radio performances, and Lafforgue made every effort to include some of these poems in this collection, which appeared in the same year, 1971, as *Décimas,* the larger anthology published in Peru. This smaller edition is also representative, however, and includes essential selections, among them the poem that gives title to the collection: "Ritmos negros del Perú," one of his earliest (1956).[12]

"Ritmos negros del Perú," which begins

> De Africa llegó mi abuela
> vestida con caracoles
> la trajeron lo'españoles
> en un barco carabela (*Ritmos,* 13)
> [My grandmother arrived from Africa
> adorned with shells,
> the Spaniards brought her over
> on a slave ship]

is, like Nancy Morejón's "Mujer negra," a signature poem. Both deal with slavery, one in the first person and the other in the third. The *abuela* who came from Africa in Santa Cruz's poem could be the generic Black woman in Morejón's. Both poems trace the Black experience from Africa to life in America. Through such poems as "Ritmos negros del Perú," Nicomedes Santa Cruz keeps alive a poetic form popular among Peruvian Blacks. Sometimes his message is painful; many of his *décimas* are *panalivios* (sad songs) or are accompanied by the sorrowful sound of the *socabón.*

Nicomedes Santa Cruz was a modern-day storyteller who not only wrote down his work but also used radio and recordings to preserve the oral tradition in the face of oppression and official disdain. Marvin Lewis gives a fine overview of several sociological and historical works that document the Black experience in Peru (Lewis, 1983, 346–50), works that show racism in one form or another to be alive and well in that country. Especially telling, for our purposes here, is his summary conclu-

sion that from all accounts, Black Peruvians find themselves still combatting lack of respect in the literary arena; he sees Santa Cruz as a victim of the age-old distinction between popular and erudite poets (Lewis,
1983, 50), a distinction that the poet himself lambasts. On more than
one occasion Santa Cruz distanced himself—and saw himself distanced—from the literary elite in his country because of discrimination
against what he did and represented.[13] Disrespecting popular poetry is
one thing, but disrespecting it because it is associated with Blacks is
quite another. Combined with the social and racial messages that Santa
Cruz later brought into his poetry, this negative, racially based deprecia-
tion of his work delayed his official inclusion in the Hispanic canon—
but endeared him to others touched by his work, like my Peruvian student and Antonio Acosta Márquez.

From the opening poems of his collection, in which he offers himself
and his poetry in service to his people, Antonio Acosta Márquez fills his
work with Black song, dance, and folklore while focusing squarely on
the toll that hard times and injustice have taken on Blacks. In this sense,
the tone of his poetry recalls some of Santa Cruz's work. Acosta
Márquez's focus on consciousness-raising is as clear as his total identification with the Blacks who are the subjects of his literature. We see this,
for example, in "Ésta es mi gente" and especially in "Canto a los
Barloventeños":

> Negritos Barloventeños
> negritos de mi país
> los de aplastada nariz
> con puro sabor costeño
> negritos como el carbón
> . . . .
> y de un gran corazón (*Yo pienso,* 18)
> [Blacks of Barlovento
> Blacks of my country
> Those coal-black
> coastal Blacks
> with flat noses
> . . . .
> and big hearts]

Both he and Santa Cruz reinforce this identification by using popular verse forms to comment on Black reality. Acosta Márquez does this poignantly in "Décimas a las madres trabajadoras" [*Décimas to the Working Mothers*] and especially in "Yo pienso aquí en donde estoy," a poem that should make even the hardened reader think twice before showing automatic disrespect toward Black people. One could use the expression "if looks could kill" to sum up the feelings conveyed in this poem about what Blacks read on White faces in racist societies.

Most of the poems in *Yo pienso aquí donde . . . estoy* open windows onto the Black mind to reveal what goes on inside. Acosta Márquez is a poet of affirmation, and his poems are frank invitations to any reader ready to be transformed. He knows he cannot hide or change his color, so others will have to change their perception if negative mindsets are to ever disappear. Acosta Márquez is as precise in his presentation of horrors endemic to the Black experience as he is aggressive in depicting Black life, festivity, and ritual in Venezuela. Marvin Lewis[14] is correct when he writes that *Yo pienso aquí donde . . . estoy* is the most recent literary assessment of Afro-Venezuelan culture from a Black perspective and that it keeps the literary dimension of Afro-Venezuelan popular culture vital. Lewis also points out that Acosta Márquez steps up his revolutionary consciousness in the second edition of his book of poems. This, together with an anti-imperialist note, leaves little doubt that he, like Nicolás Guillén, Nelson Estupiñán Bass, and Nicomedes Santa Cruz before him, places himself squarely on the side of the proletariat. And like Marcelino Arozarena in Cuba, he knows how to *cantar opinando* [state views in song].

The poet himself is a torchbearer, but he urges others to take up the torch as well. There is some of the optimism of Pilar Barrios and Geraldo Maloney in Acosta Márquez as he counsels Black youth to work hard to preserve what is theirs by preparing as best they can for the future. His poetry does not reach a high level of sophistication; he returns it to the people in forms they know and understand and with messages that chart direction. Both Santa Cruz and Antonio Acosta Márquez preserve popular forms, but a greater urgency is found in the Afro-Venezuelan's poems, especially in the later edition. Like Santa Cruz, Acosta Márquez invokes the past and is concerned with the present, but the future of Blacks in his country increasingly looms as his main preoccupation. His poetry is often a bittersweet mixture of the rhythm and reality of Black existence, of tears and laughter, of anguish and death mixed in with the vitality of life. There are lots of *minas, tam-*

bores, and *bailes,* but there are many *lamentos, velorios,* and *penas* as well. Acosta Márquez writes a very Black poetry that is also very Venezuelan. "El Negro Acosta," as he is called, is clearly more concerned with complexion than with complexity. Many of his poems immediately seem to the reader to be Black rhythms of Venezuela, which is why they recall Santa Cruz's Black rhythms of Peru. The poetry of both poets is written as if to be sung, certainly recited out loud.

Poetry, certainly in Spanish, does lend itself to the spoken word; its sound is as captivating to the ear as its structure is to the eye. From the improvisational poets of old to the Black poet-singers, rap artists, reciters, and performance poets of today, the torch is constantly being passed, ending up of late in the Grand Slam events at such places as the Nuyorican Poets Cafe in New York City. The anthology *Aloud. Voices from the Nuyorican Poets Cafe* documents the poetry recited at this place,[15] home "for the tradition that has no home but your ear" (*Aloud,* 1). Here, poets (or "slammers"), prepared to take this oral tradition into the twenty-first century, come "to read, to hear and to be heard" (*Aloud,* 15). This anthology, which includes the work of such well-known names as Victor Hernández Cruz and Sandra María Esteves, is a fascinating and useful volume, partly because it helps the reader imagine hearing aloud the voices the words represent and partly because it shows how central such new forms as rap are to the popularization of poetry, certainly poetry in the oral tradition.

Unlike the popular but structured poetry of Santa Cruz, Estupiñán Bass, Acosta Márquez, and others, much of this poetry is unstructured in the strictly formal sense; it may not rhyme but is suffused with jazz cadences and the beat of melodic recitation. Reading these performance poems, we understand what Bob Holman means when he writes that you do not have to read this book because "this book reads to you" (*Aloud,* 1). What most fascinates me about this poetry is that it is often bilingual. Some of the poets blend English and Spanish in the same poem. Miguel Algarín is partly right when he writes: "The fearlessness with which young African-American poets are now confronting languages other than English and involving themselves in the exploration of self-expression in other forms of speech is new and probably the most welcome sign of a new internationalism alive in the young African-American poets" (*Aloud,* 20). Of course, Black Americans have been exposed to and experienced Hispanic culture since the time of Langston Hughes and even before him, but the internationalism now represented by such African American poets as Tracie Morris, who are "willing to stand before live audiences and speak in Spanish" (*Aloud,* 20), does indeed represent a new development. Her "Morenita," in fact, can be read as an up-tempo, modern version of Nancy Morejón's "Mujer negra," both works tracing the ground the Black woman has covered since first brought over on "the same boat . . . Root of all evil" (*Aloud,* 102).

This latest manifestation of Black American internationalism is exciting, not just because the blending of two languages extends the possibilities of the oral tradition but also because the "fearlessness" required to step up to the podium in the first place brings to mind the heroism of Nicolás Guillén, who stepped up in the 1930s and published his *son* poems, Black musical forms set in poetry featuring Black talk and feelings, and the daring of Nicomedes Santa Cruz in the 1950s, who showed courage when he, to the consternation of some, turned his popular verse toward social and racial themes. Tracie Morris says she wrote her first poem as a personal response to a social predicament (*Aloud,* 505). The same could be said by all Black Hispanic poets.

Chapter Eleven

From Authenticity to "Authentic Space": The Emergence, Challenge, and Validity of Black Hispanic Literature

How something is seen I suppose depends on whose eyes are looking at it.
Langston Hughes

In this study I have tried to highlight some of the features that make key works of 15 Black Hispanic writers worth reading, especially to those with a Black North American perspective. I have argued that the Hispanic canon in Latin America should be expanded to include these writers not because they write "autonomous" works of literary art but in part for the opposite reason, namely, the importance their works lends to the principle of referentiality. The Black text is not hermetically sealed from reality; it has power and authority precisely because of the experience it reflects and represents. As Black Hispanic literature emerges, it will continue to offer a challenge for admission into the canon of "worthy" Hispanic texts.

Edward Mullen's recent survey of new anthologies of poetry on Black themes reveals that more Black authors are represented than in similar earlier publications from the 1930s and 1940s,[1] but representation of Black authors in general anthologies is still minimal. Howard Mancing's recent statistical survey, for example, of 100 anthologies of Spanish and Spanish American poetry published between 1940 and 1980 lists only two Black poets: Plácido and Nicolás Guillén.[2] This neglect is further dramatized when we consider that the 1940s coincide with a major period of authentic Black literary expression in Latin America, when the Black as author became as important as the Black as subject. A Marvin Lewis study covers that same period,[3] but none of the nine major Black poets he studies appears in Mancing's survey, an absence further supporting the contention that the traditional Hispanic canon in Spanish

America needs radicalizing. [Blackness continues to be as viable a concept in Latin America as it is in North America, both in literature and in criticism, and this reality is the underlying fact driving the emergence of Black Hispanic literature.] Understanding this concept is crucial—though sometimes overwhelming—for the new reader. A White student of mine once voiced displeasure because all of the Black Hispanic writers we were reading in class wrote about hardship and racism and prejudice and other such unpleasantries foreign to her experience. Black students in the class, who found all of these topics familiar to their experiences, tried to set her straight on what these writers were trying to do, but she would have none of it and remained unrepentant right up to the end of the term. She would rather they write about pleasant and less uncomfortable subjects. This student's attitude was an exception because others in the group relished the material, including feminists who saw parallels in their own "marginalized" experience.

Researchers in the field, who are constantly uncovering and bringing to light forgotten Black Hispanic texts, are enriching our knowledge about the cultural, racial, and literary mosaic of a variety of Black Hispanic areas in Latin America. Black literature in Latin America is indeed a world to discover, and not just for those outside the Afro-Hispanic field but for some inside it as well. This discovery can even reach to the countries whose experience is chronicled in these works. Michael Handelsman, for example, recently made this point about Ecuador (and, in particular, about Adalberto Ortiz and Nelson Estupiñan Bass); he believes that this country does not benefit from the insights its own Black writers bring to the national literature.[4] Handelsman's contention can be extended with variations around Latin America, where indigenous populations often get the attention due them but sometimes at the expense of Blacks whose "authentic space" (Handelsman, 9) is taken over. Handelsman rightly underscores the advantage that works by Black authors have over those by such well-known *indigenista* writers as Jorge Icaza whose novel *Huasipungo,* while teaching us something about the tragic life of Ecuador's indigenous population, is not a product of that population. Discovering such works as Adalberto Ortiz's *Juyungo* not only provides a first-rate introduction to the Black experience in all its complexity in Latin America but also lends further authenticity and enrichment to the Hispanic canon.

The concept of authenticity seems to have taken on a whole new meaning in recent years. In my first brush with it back in 1988,[5] I argued that Black Hispanic writers were no less authentic and even better models of literary Americanism than some non-Black and non-indigenous Latin American writers who have often tried, for all the right reasons, to write realistically and sincerely about the "alien cultures"[6] that the "vernacular"[7] experience in America represented to them. Later, I explored how some White writers, both students and professionals, are writing "Black" or "Indian" but for all the wrong reasons, namely, to either cash in on diversity or to deceive.[8] The point I want to make now is that only a very short step is required to move from considering a Black text as authentic and representative to considering it deserving of a place in the Hispanic canon. As well, as the courses, conferences, journals, and publications on this subject increase, it will become clearer that the emergence of Black Hispanic literature marks the birth and growth of a discipline while providing valid insights into Latin America as a whole.

Black Hispanic writers do indeed represent alternate voices in Latin America, but their "minority" discourse has its own power and authority, which it is up to us to see. For example, Keith Ellis identified the coverage of large sweeps of history as one of the features of the work of such foremost twentieth-century Spanish American writers and artists as Pablo Neruda, Alejo Carpentier, Juan Rulfo, Gabriel García Márquez, and Diego Rivera.[9] But we can extend this list to include Black Hispanic writers who also tell the big story of their countries or regions or of the entire New World, often in works as unique as those of these renowned artists; they have been chroniclers of their own time and have remembered the past while looking to the future. They clearly consider themselves spokespersons who, like the early *cronista* Bernal Díaz del Castillo, tried to write "true" history. Like Pablo Neruda, the leading poetic chronicler of our time, such Black Hispanic writers as Manuel Zapata Olivella, Carlos Guillermo Wilson, and Nicolás Guillén also present the other side of history by giving voice to the forgotten ones.

Black Hispanic writers bring to the canon the same theme of the "struggle for justice in the New World" popularized foremost by Neruda.[10] Black slavery is certainly related to that theme and to that struggle, but because it is not well represented in Neruda's famous epic *Canto general* (1950), it is profitable to turn to such works as Manuel Zapata Olivella's novel *Changó, el gran putas* (1983), to Nicolás Guillén's *El diario que a diario* (1972), or to Cubena's *Los nietos de Felicidad Dolores* (1990) for this big story, especially when we recognize that there are few Blacks in Neruda's *Canto general,* one of the poem's "most glaring omissions."[11] One cannot expect that Neruda should have written about

Blacks to the same extent as Guillén or Zapata Olivella because his experience clearly is not theirs; his *Canto general* is a "general" song, but one limited by the Chilean author's own personal experience, interest, and vindictive mission.

Understandably, Neruda focused on the original Indian inhabitants of America, especially because he started his poem in Mexico, where he spent three years surrounded by the work of his friends, the Mexican muralists Rivera, Siqueiros, and Orozco, who glorified Mexico's Indian heritage, and because during his visit to Macchu Picchu, he felt "Chilean, Peruvian, and American."[12] Also understandable is the enormous presence of Southern Chile ("mi tierra" ["my land"]) in his long poem, as the original idea was to write a *Canto general de Chile* [*General Song of Chile*], which he did but then incorporated into the larger work. Neruda was writing out of ideology, geography, and experience but little of it had anything to do with Blacks, which is why students should read *Canto general* in tandem certainly with Zapata Olivella's *Changó, el gran putas*. Zapata Olivella's perspective is Afrocentric, but his work is no less valid than other attempts, both in this century and earlier, to write "The Great Song of America" (Brotherston, 27).

Black Hispanic literature is emerging at a good time. These days, students are looking for something exciting and new. Black Hispanic literature is not new, but it is getting more attention and does indeed fill a need in the current movement toward diversity; it proves that authors do not have to be, as the cliché goes, White, male, European, and dead to be worth studying. Black Hispanic literature always has had the power. It is up to us to see that it is taken seriously. By organizing the chapters in this study around such writers who came into prominence in the 1980s and 1990s as Carlos Guillermo Wilson, Quince Duncan, Blas Jiménez, Norberto James, Gerardo Maloney, Antonio Acosta Márquez, and Nancy Morejón, as well as around honored members of the Black Hispanic canon such as Juan Francisco Manzano, Pilar Barrios, Nicolás Guillén, Juan Pablo Sojo, Adalberto Ortiz, Nicomedes Santa Cruz, Nelson Estupiñán Bass and Manuel Zapata Olivella, I believe I have included what Henry Louis Gates Jr. would call the "crucially central" authors and the "essential texts" indispensable in a discussion of this kind.

Notes and References

Chapter One

1. Theodore O. Mason Jr., "The Academic Critic and Power: Trends in Contemporary Afro-American Literature and Criticism," in *Culture/Criticism/Ideology. Proceedings of the Northeastern University Center for Literary Studies,* vol. 4, ed. Stuart Peterfreund (Boston: Northeastern University Press, 1987), 48. Hereafter cited in text as Mason.

2. David William Foster, *Alternate Voices in the Contemporary Latin American Narrative* (Columbia: University of Missouri Press, 1985), 1.

3. J. Kubayanda, "Minority Discourse and the African Collective: Some Examples from Latin American and Caribbean Literature," *Cultural Critique* 6 (Spring 1987): 119. Here Kubayanda cites Roberto González Echevarría, *The Voice of the Masters: Writing and Authority in Modern Latin American Literature* (Austin: University of Texas Press, 1985), xvi.

4. Keith Ellis, "Images of Black People in the Poetry of Nicolás Guillén," *Afro-Hispanic Review* 7, nos. 1–3 (1988): 19–22, where he discusses obfuscating trends in the criticism of Guillén's work.

5. Yvonne Captain, "Writing for the Future: Afro-Hispanism in a Global, Critical Context," *Afro-Hispanic Review* 13, no. 1 (1994): 5. Hereafter cited in text as Captain.

6. See Richard Jackson, "Afro-Hispanic Literature: The New Frontier of Avant-Garde Criticism," *Callaloo* 12, no. 1 (1989): 255–60; "Afro-Hispanic Literature: Recent Trends in Criticism," *Afro-Hispanic Review* 7, nos. 1–3 (1988): 32–35; and "Recent Trends in Afro-Spanish American Literary Criticism," in *The Afro-Spanish American Author II: The 1980s: An Annotated Bibliography of Recent Criticism* (West Cornwall, CT: Locust Hill Press, 1989), xiii–xviii.

7. See Vera Kutzinski, "Re-Reading Nicolás Guillén: An Introduction," *Nicolás Guillén: A Special Issue,* ed. Vera Kutzinski (*Callaloo* 10, no. 2 [1987]):161–67. Kutzinski and Jonathan Tittler claim that Black writers are more concerned with complexity than with complexion.

8. See note 7.

9. See some of the recent studies on these authors annotated in Richard Jackson, *The Afro-Spanish American Author II: The 1980s.* Also see the third volume, forthcoming.

10. See Millicent A. Bolden, "Conversación entre Nelson Estupiñán Bass y Millicent A. Bolden," *Afro-Hispanic Review* 7, no. 3 (1989): 16.

11.   Recent writings by Guillermo Cabrera Infante and especially by Carlos Moore and Linda Howe have fueled this particular controversy. For more on this issue, see chapter 3.

12.   See Richard L. Jackson, *The Afro-Spanish American Author: An Annotated Bibliography of Criticism* (New York: Garland Publishing Co., 1980), xiii–xiv.

13.   See G.R. Coulthard, *Race and Colour in Caribbean Literature* (London: Oxford University Press, 1962), 5.

14.   Janheinz Jahn, *A History of Neo-African Literature,* trans. Oliver Coburn and Ursula Lehrburger (London: Faber and Faber, Ltd., 1968).

15.   See William Luis, ed., *Voices from Under: Black Narrative in Latin America and the Caribbean* (Westport, CT: Greenwood Press, 1984), 250.

16.   See Antonio Olliz Boyd, "The Concept of Black Aesthetics as Seen in Selected Works of Three Latin American Writers: Machado de Assis, Nicolás Guillén, and Adalberto Ortiz" (Ph.D. diss., Stanford University, 1975).

17.   See J. Kubayanda, "Minority Discourse." Also see his *The Poet's Africa: Africanness in the Poetry of Nicolás Guillén and Aimé Césaire* (New York: Greenwood Press, 1990).

18.   See Ian Smart, *Central American Writers of West Indian Origin: A New Hispanic Literature* (Washington, D.C.: Three Continents Press, 1984).

19.   Alan Persico, "Quince Duncan's *Los cuatro espejos:* Time, History, and a New Novel," *Afro-Hispanic Review* 10, no. 1 (1991).

20.   Alan Persico, "Ramón Díaz Sánchez: Primitive or Creator," *Afro-Hispanic Review* 5, nos. 1–3 (1986): 13.

21.   See Vera Kutzinski, *Sugar's Secrets: Race and the Erotics of Cuban Nationalism* (Charlottesville: University Press of Virginia, 1993), 13.

22.   For Guillén's remarks on this Puerto Rican *negrista* poet, see Laurence Prescott, "A Conversation with Nicolás Guillén," *Nicolás Guillén: A Special Issue,* ed. Vera Kutzinski, 353.

23.   See Ian Smart, "The Literary World of Quince Duncan: An Interview," *CLA Journal* 28, no. 3 (1985): 286.

24.   See, for example, her *Para una semiótica de la mulatez* (Madrid: Ediciones José Porrúa Turanzas, 1990).

25.   I consider the works that I discuss here to be representative only because no list or canon should be fixed, authoritative, and unchanging, thus permanently institutionalizing one group of writers over another. To quote Catharine Stimpson in reference to Harold Bloom's list in his new book *The Western Canon: The Books and School of the Ages* (New York: Harcourt Brace, 1994): "The mistake would be to take the list and say, 'This is the list.' " In Rebecca Mead, "The Next Big Lit-Crit-Snit," *New York* 15 (August 1994): 42. Even Bloom claims his list tells readers "neither what to read nor how to read it, only what [he has] read and think[s] worthy of rereading." In Cathy Hainer, "Harold Bloom's Literary Canon Explodes," *USA Today,* 11 October 1994, 6D.

Chapter Two

1. Francisco Calcagno, *Poetas de color (Plácido, Manzano, Rodríguez, Echemendía, Silveira, Medina)*, 4th ed. (Havana: Imprenta Mercantil de los Herederos de Santiago, 1887).

2. Roberto Friol, *Suite para Juan Francisco Manzano* (Havana: Editorial Arte y Literatura, 1977).

3. Vicente Caraballo, *El negro Obeso (apuntes biográficos) y escritos varios* (Bogotá: Editorial A.B.C., 1943).

4. Laurence Prescott, *Candelario Obeso y la iniciación de la poesía negra en Colombia* (Bogotá: Instituto Caro y Cuervo, 1985).

5. Concha Peña, *Gaspar Octavio Hernández. "Poeta del Pueblo"* (Panama: Imprenta Nacional, 1953).

6. Ivan Augusto Gómez, "Estudio de la poesía de Gaspar Octavio Hernández. Acompañado de un intento de análisis estilístico de su 'Poema del pasado, del presente, y del porvenir: Cristo y la mujer de Sichar' " (Ph.D. diss., University of Panama, 1956–1957).

7. Gaspar Octavio Hernández, *Obras selectas,* ed. Octavio Augusto Hernández (Panama: Imprenta Nacional, 1966), 111.

8. *The Life and Poems of a Cuban Slave: Juan Francisco Manzano 1797–1854,* ed. Edward J. Mullen (Hamden, Conn.: Archon Books, 1981), 217.

9. Sylvia Molloy, "From Serf to Self: The *Autobiografía* de Juan Francisco Manzano," *Modern Language Notes, Hispanic Edition* 104, no. 2 (1989): 393–417.

10. Leopoldo Horrego Estuch, *Martín Morúa Delgado. Vida y mensaje* (Havana: Comisión Nacional del Centenario de Martín Morúa Delgado, 1959).

11. Nicolás Guillén, "Martín Morúa Delgado," *Bohemia* (1 September 1949), reprinted in Martín Morúa Delgado, *La familia Unzúazu* (Havana: Editorial Arte y Literatura, 1975), 245–65.

12. Angel Augier, *Nicolás Guillén. Estudio biográfico-crítico* (1947; reprint, Havana: Ediciones Unión, 1984).

13. Ronna Smith Newman, "Life and Works of Adalberto Ortiz" (Ph.D. diss., Northwestern University, 1981).

14. Pilar Barrios, "Autobiografía," in *Piel negra* (Montevideo: Nuestra Raza, 1947), 12–13. First published in Ildefonso Pereda Valdés, ed., *Antología de la poesía negra americana* (Santiago: Ediciones Ercilla, 1936), 129.

15. Yvonne Captain-Hidalgo, *The Culture of Fiction in the Works of Manuel Zapata Olivella* (Columbia: University of Missouri Press, 1993).

16. Frederick S. Stimson, *Cuba's Romantic Poet. The Story of Plácido* (Chapel Hill: University of North Carolina Press, 1964).

17. See Frederick S. Stimson and Humberto E. Robles, eds., *Los poemas más representativos de Plácido (edición crítica)* (Chapel Hill: Estudios de Hispanófila, 1976), 128–31.

18. Elba Birmingham-Pokorny, "Interview with Dr. Carlos Guillermo Wilson," in *Denouncement and Reaffirmation of the Afro-Hispanic Identity in Carlos Guillermo Wilson's Works* (Miami: Ediciones Universal, 1993), 15–25.

19. Norberto James, "First person Singular?" in *Being America: Essays on Art, Literature and Identity from Latin America,* ed. Rachel Weiss with Alan West (Fredonia, NY: White Pine Press, 1991), 51–58.

20. Laurence Prescott, "A Conversation with Nicolás Guillén," in *Nicolás Guillén: A Special Issue,* ed. Vera Kutzinski, (*Callaloo* 10, no. 2 [1987]: 352–54).

21. Nicolás Guillén, *Páginas vueltas. Memorias* (Havana: Ediciones Unión, 1982).

22. Orlando Castellanos, "Con Nicolás Guillén," *Casa de las Américas* 30, no. 176 (1989): 3–7.

23. Nancy Morejón, "Conversación con Nicolás Guillén," *Recopilación de textos sobre Nicolás Guillén* (Havana: Casa de las Américas, 1974), 31–61.

24. Keith Ellis, "Conversation with Nicolás Guillén," *Jamaican Journal* 7, nos. 1–2 (1973): 77–79.

25. Robert Chrisman, "Langston Hughes: Six letters to Nicolás Guillén," trans. Carmen Alegría, *The Black Scholar* 16, no. 4 (1985): 54–60.

26. Manuel Zapata Olivella, *He visto la noche* (Bogotá: Editorial Andes, 1953; Medellín: Editorial Bedout, 1969, 1974).

27. Yvonne Captain-Hidalgo, "Conversación con el doctor Manuel Zapata Olivella, Bogotá, 1980, 1983)," *Afro-Hispanic Review* 4, no. 1 (1985): 26–32.

28. Ronna Smith Newman, "Conversación con Adalberto Ortiz," *Cultura* (Quito, May–August 1983): 189–210.

29. Michael Walker, "Appendix," in "The Black Social Identity in Selected Novels of Nelson Estupiñán Bass and Adalberto Ortiz" (Ph.D. diss., University of California–Riverside, (1977): 188–94.

30. Stanley Cyrus, "Ethnic Ambivalence and Afro-Hispanic Novelists," *Afro-Hispanic Review* 1, no. 1 (1982): 29–32.

31. Antonio Planells, "Adalberto Ortiz: el hombre y la creación literaria," *Afro-Hispanic Review* 4, nos. 2 and 3 (1985): 29–33.

32. Henry Richards, "Entrevista con Nelson Estupiñán Bass," *Afro-Hispanic Review* 2, no. 1 (1983): 29–30, and "Entrevista con Nelson Estupiñán Bass," *Afro-Hispanic Review* 4, nos. 2 and 3 (1985): 34–35.

33. Millicent Bolden, "Conversación entre Nelson Estupiñán Bass y Millicent Bolden," *Afro-Hispanic Review* 7, no. 3 (1989): 14–16.

34. Rosemary Geisdorfer Feal, "Entrevista con Luz Argentina Chiriboga," *Afro-Hispanic Review* 12, no. 2 (1993): 16. Also see Carol Beane, "Entrevista con Luz Argentina Chiriboga," *Afro-Hispanic Review* 12, no. 2 (1993): 17–23.

35. Lorna Williams, "Entrevista con Cristina Rodríguez Cabral," *Afro-Hispanic Review* 14, no. 2 (1995): 57–63.

36. Laurence Prescott, "Remembering Jorge Artel (1909, Cartagena–1994, Barranquilla)," *Afro-Hispanic Review* 15, no. 1 (1996): 1. Prescott plans to title his book on Artel *Without Hatreds or Fears: Jorge Artel and the Struggle for Black Literary Expression in Colombia.*

37. Antonio Acosta Márquez, "Palabras del autor. 'Un país donde los nuevos valores somos marginados,'" *Yo pienso aquí donde . . . estoy* (Medellín: Editorial Cascabel, 1977), xvi–xvii.

38. Elena Poniatowska, "Habla el peruano Nicomedes Santa Cruz," *¡Siempre!,* 14 August 1974: 39–41, 70.

39. Nicomedes Santa Cruz, "Mis primeras décimas," *Décimas y poemas, antología* (Lima: Campodónio Ediciones, S. A., 1971), 11–17.

40. Rafael Rodríguez, "Nancy Morejón en su Habana," *Areíto* 8, no. 32 (1983): 23–25.

41. Magdalena García-Pinto, "Entrevista con Pedro Pérez Sarduy en Columbia, Missouri, en marzo de 1993," *Afro-Hispanic Review* 13, no. 1 (1994): 23–33.

42. Pedro Pérez Sarduy, "Open Letter to Carlos Moore," *Afro-Hispanic Review* 9, nos. 1–3 (1990): 25–29.

43. Adalberto Ortiz, "Negritude in Latin American Culture," in *Blacks in Hispanic Literature. Critical Essays,* ed. and trans. Miriam deCosta (Port Washington, NY: Kennikat Press, 1977), 74–82.

44. See Richard Jackson, "Hispanic Black Criticism and the North American Perspective," *Black Writers and Latin America: Cross-Cultural Affinities* (Washington, D.C.: Howard University Press, in press).

45. Luis Freire, "La sirena popular de Gregorio," *Runa* 6 (1977): 33–35.

46. Carlos Arturo Truque, "My Testimony," trans. June M. Legge, *Afro-Hispanic Review* 1, no. 1 (1982): 17–22. Hereafter cited in text as Truque.

Chapter Three

1. Recent books appearing in the 1990s on Manzano, Guillén, and Morejón include Ian Isidore Smart's *Nicolás Guillén: Popular Poet of the Caribbean* (Columbia: University of Missouri Press, 1990), hereafter cited in text as Smart; Josaphat B. Kubayanda's *The Poet's Africa: Africanness in the Poetry of Nicolás Guillén and Aimé Césaire* (New York: Greenwood Press, 1990) and Clement A. White, *Decoding the Word: Nicolás Guillén as Maker and Debunker of Myth* (Miami: Ediciones Universal, 1993). William Luis's recent discussion of Manzano in his *Literary Bondage: Slavery in Cuban Narrative* (Austin: University of Texas Press, 1990), hereafter cited as Luis in text, is very useful, as is Lorna Williams's in *The Representation of Slavery in Cuban Fiction* (Columbia: University of Missouri Press, 1994), hereafter cited as Williams in text. Also see Mercedes Rivas, *Literatura y esclavitud en la novela cubana del siglo XIX* (Sevilla: Escuela de Estudios Hispano-Americanos de Sevilla, 1990), hereafter cited as Rivas in text. On Nancy Morejón, see Vera Kutzinski, *Sugar's Secrets: Race and the Erotics of*

Cuban Nationalism (Charlottesville: University Press of Virginia, 1993), hereafter cited as Kutzinski 1993 in text. Also see *Nancy Morejón. A Special Issue,* ed.
Edward Mullen (*Afro-Hispanic Review* 15, no. 1 [1996]), and a collection of
essays on Morejón, some new and others previously published, currently being
compiled by Miriam DeCosta.

   2.   Julio Finn, *Voices of Negritude* (London: Quartet Books, 1988), 169.
   3.   Nicolás Guillén wrote several poems on slavery although none of
them, in Vera Kutzinski's view, gives the Cuban woman her due. See *Kutzinski
1993,* especially chapter 6, "Sublime Masculinity."
   4.   In Nicolás Guillén, *Obra poética 1958–1972,* 2 vols. (Havana: Editorial Arte y Literatura, 1974), hereafter cited in text as I or II.
   5.   See "The Turning Point: The Blackening of Nicolás Guillén and the
Impact of his *Motivos de son*" in my *Black Writers in Latin America* (Albuquerque:
University of New Mexico Press, 1979), 80–92, and "The Afrocriollo Movement Revisited" in my *Black Literature and Humanism in Latin America* (Athens:
University of Georgia Press, 1988), 20–31. Also see Edward J. Mullen, "Some
Early Reading of *Motivos de son,*" *Romance notes* 39, no. 2 (1992): 221–30, for a
recent discussion of the early critical reaction to these poems.
   6.   See Jill Ann Netchinsky, "Engendering a Cuban Literature: Nineteenth-Century Antislavery Narrative (Manzano, Suárez y Romero, Gómez de
Avellaneda, A. Zambrana)" (Ph.D. diss., Yale University, 1986), 41.
   7.   One has to see Manzano's reluctance as a signal or as a restraint.
Angelo Costanzo cautions the reader of slave narratives to look for such subtle
devices as character disguises and masks in descriptions of personal incidents so
that the true story that the slave attempted to communicate to the world can
be revealed. See Angelo Costanzo, "The Narrative of Archibald Monteith, A
Jamaican Slave," *Callaloo* 13, no. 1 (1990): 118.
   8.   See Ivan Schulman, "Juan Francisco Manzano or the Resurrection of
a Dead Soul," *Review* 31 (January–April 1981): 60–61.
   9.   See Richard Jackson, *The Black Image in Latin American Literature*
(Albuquerque: University of New Mexico Press, 1976) 95. Also see "Slave
Poetry and Slave Narrative: Juan Francisco Manzano and Black Autobiography" and "Slave Societies and the Free Black Writer: José Manuel Valdés and
'Plácido' " in my *Black Writers in Latin America,* 25–35; 36–44. Also see my
essay "Slavery, Racism and Autobiography in Two Early Black Writers: Juan
Francisco Manzano and Martín Morúa Delgado" in *Voices from Under: Black
Narrative in Latin America and the Caribbean* ed. William Luis (Westport, CT.:
Greenwood Press, 1984), 55–64.
   10.   See Roberto Friol, *Suite para Juan Francisco Manzano* (Havana: Editorial Arte y Literatura, 1977), for an excellent compilation of documentation on
and opinion about Manzano's life and works.
   11.   Plácido's accusations here might have been contrived because he
never signed his confession. See Luis, *Literary Bondage,* 17.

12. This quotation is taken from an open letter that Del Monte wrote for publication in a Paris newspaper in 1844. For a discussion of the letter, Del Monte's true feelings about Blacks, and his "use" of Manzano, see Sylvia Molloy, "From Serf to Self: The Autobiography of Juan Francisco Manzano," *Modern Language Notes. Hispanic Issue* 104, no. 2 (1989): 393–417.

13. See J. Kubayanda, "Hispanic Humanism and Nineteenth-Century Cuban Blacks: An Historico-Literary Perspective," *Plantation Society* 1, no. 3 (1981): 343–63.

14. William Luis's work gives a fascinating account of the multiple versions of Manzano's autobiography: Manzano's own manuscript; José Luciano Franco's slightly modified version of it; Suárez y Romero's version corresponding to the Calgagno fragments; Madden's version, which could be Suárez y Romero's; and the Azcárate notebook. All of these differ from Manzano's actual life. Luis's work sheds new light on all of this and especially on the Madden version, which turns out to be neither Madden's nor Manzano's. See his *Literary Bondage,* 93–100. Also see his article "Autobiografía del esclavo Juan Francisco Manzano: versión de Suárez y Romero" in *Memorias del 26 Congreso del Instituto Internacional de Literatura Iberoamericana,* ed. Raquel Chang-Rodriguez y Gabriella de Beer (Hanover: Ediciones del Norte, 1989).

15. Keith Ellis, *Cuba's Nicolás Guillén. Poetry and Ideology* (Toronto: University of Toronto Press, 1983), 201, hereafter cited as Ellis in text.

16. Luis F. González-Cruz, "Nature and the Black Reality in Three Caribbean Poets: A New Look at the Concept of Negritude," *Perspectives on Contemporary Literature* 5 (1979): 144.

17. Vera Kutzinski, *Against the American Grain: Myth and History in William Carlos Williams, Jay Wright, and Nicolás Guillén* (Baltimore: The Johns Hopkins University Press, 1987), 172; hereafter cited in text as Kutzinski 1987.

18. Translated and reprinted in Vera Kutzinski, *Against the American Grain,* 165.

19. Angel Augier, *Nicolás Guillén. Estudio biográfico-crítico* (Havana: Ediciones Union, 1984), 514.

20. For several examples and translations see Kutzinski 1987, 189–91, and her recent translation of the complete work into English as *The Daily Daily* (Berkeley: University of California Press, 1989).

21. Roberto González Echevarría, "Guillén as Baroque: Meaning in *Motivos de son,*" *Nicolás Guillén: A Special Issue,* ed. Vera Kutzinski (*Callaloo* 10, no. 2 [1987]): 302–17.

22. See Richard L. Jackson, "Nancy Morejón, the 'New Woman' in Cuba, and the First Generation of Black Writers of the Revolution," in *Black Writers and Latin America: Cross-Cultural Affinities* (Washington: Howard University Press, in press). Also see *Nancy Morejón. A Special Issue,* ed. Edward J. Mullen (*Afro-Hispanic Review* 15, no. 1 [1996]).

23. Elizabeth Fox-Genovese, "A Manifold Challenge," review of Harriet A. Jacobs's *Incidents in the Life of a Slave Girl, Written by Herself,* ed. Jean Fagan

Yellin (Cambridge: Harvard University Press, 1987), *Times Literary Supplement,* 4 December 1987, 1340.

24. Linda Howe, "Nancy Morejón's 'Mujer negra': Rereading Afrocentric Hermeneutics, Rewriting Gender," *The Journal of Afro-Latin American Studies and Literatures* 1, no. 1 (1993–1994):95–107.

25. G. Cabrera Infante, "Nicolás Guillén: Poet and Partisan," *Review: Latin American Literature and Arts* 42 (January–June 1990): 31–33.

26. Carlos Moore, *Castro, the Blacks and Africa* (Berkeley: University of California Press, 1989).

27. Morejón must be making her case pretty well. In August 1993, she organized a conference in Havana on Afro-Cuban culture.

28. Nancy Morejón, *Parajes de una época* (Havana: Editorial Letras Cubanas, 1979), 18–20.

29. Nancy Morejón, "Mujer negra," *Casa de las Américas* 15, no. 88 (1975): 19–20.

30. Claudette Rose Green-Williams, "Re-Writing the History of the Afro-Cuban Woman: Nancy Morejón's 'Mujer negra,' " *Afro-Hispanic Review* 8, no. 3 (1989).

31. Miriam de Costa Willis, "Nancy Morejón and the Concept of Black Poetry," unpublished essay.

32. William Luis makes the same comment. In conversation with Elio Ruiz he says: about a book called "En *¿Quiénes escriben en Cuba?* de Bernard y Pola me sorprendió mucho que a pesar de que se recogen entrevistas con escritores de fama nacional, no aparece ni el nombre de ella [Nancy Morejón] ni el de Guillén" [In *Writers in Cuba* by Bernard and Pola I was surprised that in a collection of interviews with nationally known writers, neither her name [Nancy Morejón] nor that of Guillén appears]. William Luis, "Cultura afrocubana en la Revolución: Entrevista a Elio Ruiz," *Afro-Hispanic Review* 13, no. 1 (1994): 44.

33. See Ingrid Peritz, "Still Faithful to Fidel," *Gazette* (Montreal), 27 August 1994, B3.

Chapter Four

1. Marvin Lewis, *Ethnicity and Identity in Contemporary Afro-Venezuelan Literature. A Culturalist Approach* (Columbia: University of Missouri Press, 1992), 10, hereafter cited in text as Lewis.

2. Juan Pablo Sojo, *Nochebuena negra* (Caracas: Editorial Elite, 1943; Caracas: Monte Avila, 1972). Hereafter cited in text as *NN.*

3. Juan Pablo Sojo, *Temas y apuntes afro-venezolanos* (Caracas: Tipografía La Nación, 1943). Hereafter cited in text as *Temas.*

4. Richard Jackson, "Miscegenation and Personal Choice in Two Contemporary Novels of Continental Spanish America," *Hispania* 50, no. 1 (1967): 86–88.

5.   Richard Jackson, *The Black Image in Latin American Literature* (Albuquerque: University of New Mexico Press, 1976), 116.

Chapter Five

1.   See Richard L. Jackson, "Adalberto Ortiz and his Black Ecuadorian Classic," *Black Writers in Latin America* (Albuquerque: University of New Mexico Press, 1979), 122–29.
2.   See Adalberto Ortiz, *Juyungo,* trans. Susan Hill and Jonathan Titler (Washington: Three Continents Press, 1982). Hereafter cited in text as *Juyungo.*
3.   See Richard L. Jackson, "Modern Black Heroism," *Black Literature and Humanism in Latin America* (Athens: University of Georgia Press, 1988), 38–49. Hereafter cited in text as Jackson 1988.
4.   This novel has recently been translated by Ian Smart as *Pastrana's Last River* (Washington: Afro-Hispanic Institute, 1993). To Smart's credit, he translates from the first edition. All quotations in English are taken from this edition. Hereafter cited in text as *River.* This is the third novel by Nelson Estupiñán Bass now available in English; the other two are *When the Guyacans Were in Bloom* and *Curfew,* both translated by Henry Richards.
5.   See Nelson Estupiñán Bass, *El último río* (Quito: Casa de la Cultura Ecuatoriana, 1966).
6.   See Fernando Tijanero Villamar, "Una historia de pasión," Nelson Estupiñán Bass, *El último río* (Quito: Casa de la Cultura Ecuatoriana, 1966), 9–14.
7.   See Edna N. Sims, " 'Is There a Battle of the Sexes in *El último río?*' A Comparative Study," *Middle Atlantic Writers Association Review* 3, no. 1 (June 1988): 19–22.
8.   Henry Richards, "Nelson Estupiñán Bass on *El último río,*" *Afro-Hispanic Review* 10, no. 1 (1991): 23. Hereafter cited in text as Richards 1991.
9.   See Angela Escrivá-Carnicer, "Crossing the Last River: The Search for Identity in Nelson Estupiñán Bass's *El último río,*" *Diáspora* 1 (1991): 52–62.
10.   See Henry Richards, "Narrative Strategies in Nelson Estupiñán Bass's *El último río,*" *Afro-Hispanic Review* (January 1982): 11–15.
11.   See Myrna Kostash, "You Don't Check Your Colour at the Door," *Globe and Mail* (Toronto), 9 May 1994, A19.
12.   See Richard Jackson, *The Black Image in Latin American Literature* (Albuquerque: University of New Mexico Press, 1976), 107–9.
13.   Millicent A. Bolden, "Conversación entre Nelson Estupiñán Bass y Millicent A. Bolden," *Afro-Hispanic Review* 7, no. 3 (1989): 16. Hereafter cited in text as Bolden.
14.   See Abdias do Nascimento, *Cadernos brasileiros* 10.47 (1968): 5, and "The Negro Theater in Brazil," *African Forum* 2 (1967): 44.
15.   Nelson Estupiñán Bass, *El último río,* 2d ed. (Quito: Casa de la Cultura Económica, 1980), 141.

Chapter Six

1. Yvonne Captain-Hidalgo, *The Culture of Fiction in the Works of Manuel Zapata Olivella* (Columbia: University of Missouri Press, 1994), hereafter cited as Captain-Hidalgo in text.
2. For an excellent new scholastic edition in Spanish, see Manuel Zapata Olivella, *Chambacú, corral de negros,* ed. José Luis Díaz Granados (Bogotá: Rei Andes, 1990). Also see Jonathan Tittler, *Chambacú: Black Slum* (Pittsburgh: Latin American Literary Review Press, 1989).
3. For a new edition, see Manuel Zapata Olivella, *Changó, el gran putas* (Bogotá: Rei Andes, 1992).
4. This work was first published in French as *Lève toi mulâtre!* (Paris: Payot, 1987) and later appeared in Spanish as *¡Levántate mulato!* (Bogotá: Rei Andes, 1990). Hereafter cited in text as *LM.*
5. See Nicolás Guillén, *Páginas vueltas. Memorias* (Havana: Ediciones Unión, 1982).
6. Roberto González Echevarría, "Guillén as Baroque: Meaning in *Motivos de son,*" *Nicolás Guillen: A Special Issue,* ed. Vera K. Kutzinski, (*Callaloo* 10, no. 2 [1987]): 302–17.
7. In James Weldon Johnson, "Native African Races and Cultures," reprinted in *Langston Hughes Review* 8, nos. 1–2 (1989): 31. Hereafter cited in text as Johnson.
8. James Brooke, "Long Neglected, Colombia's Blacks Win Changes," *The New York Times,* 29 March 1994, A3.

Chapter Seven

1. Shirley Jackson, "The Special Gift of Literature," *Monographic Review/Revista monográfica* (1985): 83–89.
2. Stephanie Davis-Lett, "Blacks and Criollism: A Curious Relationship," *College Language Association Journal* 24, no. 2 (1980): 131–49.
3. Richard Jackson, *Black Literature and Humanism in Latin America* (Athens: University of Georgia Press, 1988). Hereafter cited in text as Jackson 1988.
4. Pilar Barrios, *Piel negra. Poesías (1917–1947)* (Montevideo: Nuestra Raza, 1947), 51. Hereafter cited in text as *PN.*
5. Caroll Young, "The New Voices of Afro-Uruguay," *Afro-Hispanic Review* 14, no. 1 (1995): 58.
6. Nathanial C. Nash, "Uruguay Is on Notice: Blacks Want Recognition," *New York Times,* 7 May 1993, A4. Hereafter cited in text as Nash.
7. Alberto Britos Serrat, ed., *Antología de poetas negros uruguayos* (Montevideo: Ediciones Mundo Afro, 1991).
8. See "Afro-Uruguayan Poetry," *Afro-Hispanic Review* 12, no. 2 (1993): 37–47.

9. Ian I. Smart, "Popular Black Intellectualism in Gerardo Maloney's *Juega vivo,*" *Afro-Hispanic Review* 5, nos. 1–3 (1986): 43.

10. Gerardo Maloney, *Juega vivo* (Panama: Formato Dieciseis, 1984), 75. Hereafter cited in text as *JV.*

11. Ian I. Smart, *Central American Writers of West Indian Origin. A New Hispanic Literature* (Washington, D.C.: Three Continents Press, 1984), 90–91.

Chapter Eight

1. See Ian Smart, *Central American Writers of West Indian Origin: A New Hispanic Literature* (Washington, D.C.: Three Continents Press, 1984).

2. Ian Smart, "*Changó, El Gran Putas* as Liberation Literature," *CLA Journal* 35, no. 1 (1991): 21.

3. See Claire Smith, "When Race Alters the Public's Perceptions," *New York Times,* 16 March 1992, C8.

4. Quince Duncan, *Kimbo* (San José: Editorial Costa Rica, 1989), 49. Hereafter cited in text as *Kimbo.*

5. In Ian Smart, "The Literary World of Quince Duncan: An Interview," *CLA Journal* 28, no. 3 (1985): 290.

6. Ellis Cose, "Caught Between Two Worlds," *Newsweek,* 11 July 1994, 28.

7. See Richard L. Jackson, "Return to the Origins: The Afro-Costa Rican Literature of Quince Duncan," *Black Literature and Latin America* (Albuquerque: University of New Mexico Press, 1979), 171–79.

8. Quince Duncan, *Los cuatro espejos* (San José: Editorial Costa Rica, 1973), 1. Hereafter cited in text as *LCE.*

9. From an O.J. Simpson autobiography, reprinted in Andrew Murr et al., "Day and Night," *Newsweek,* 29 August 1994, 43–49.

10. See Lorna V. Williams, "Carlos Guillermo Wilson and the Dialectics of Ethnicity in Panama," *Afro-Hispanic Review* 4, nos. 2–3 (1985): 15.

11. Barbara Solow, in a letter to the editor, *New York Times,* 8 November 1990, A34.

12. Elba Birmingham-Pokorny, "The Afro-Hispanic Woman's Role in the Re-writing of Her History in Carlos Guillermo Wilson's *Los nietos de Felicidad Dolores,*" *Proceedings of The Image(s) of The Afro-Hispanic Woman in Latin American Literature and Culture,* ed. Elba Birmingham-Pokorny (Magnolia: Southern Arkansas University, 1990), 39–50.

13. Carlos Guillermo Wilson (Cubena), *Los nietos de Felicidad Dolores* (Miami: Ediciones Universal, 1990), 77. Hereafter cited in text as *Nietos.*

14. Elba Birmingham-Pokorny, "Interview with Dr. Carlos Guillermo Wilson," *Denouncement and Reaffirmation of the Afro-Hispanic Identity in Carlos Guillermo Wilson's Work,* ed. Elba Birmingham-Pokorny (Miami: Ediciones Universal, 1993), 19. Hereafter cited in text as Birmingham-Pokorny.

Chapter Nine

1. Racist and derogatory term applied to Black Dominicans of English-speaking West Indian origin.
2. See Norberto James, "First Person Singular?" in *Being America: Essays on Art, Literature and Identity from Latin America,* ed. Rachel Weiss with Alan West (Fredonia, NY: White Pine Press, 1991), 58. Hereafter cited in text as James.
3. See Howard W. French, "A Dominican's 2 Burdens: Haiti and Balaguer," *New York Times,* 4 April 1994, A4.
4. In James J. Davis, "Entrevista con el dominicano Norberto James Rawlings," *Afro-Hispanic Review* 6, no. 2 (1987): 18. Hereafter cited in text as Davis 1987.
5. Blas R. Jiménez, *Exigencias de un cimarrón (en sueños)* (Santo Domingo: Editora Taller, 1987), 101.
6. Blas R. Jiménez, *Caribe africano en despertar* (Santo Domingo: Edicions Nuevas Rutas, 1984). Hereafter cited in text as *Caribe.*
7. Norberto James, *Sobre la Marcha,* in his *Hago constar (poemas—1969–1972)* (Santo Domingo: Editora Taller, 1983), 9–49. Hereafter cited in text as *Marcha.*
8. Blas Jiménez, *Aquí . . . otro español* (Santo Domingo: Editorial Incoco, 1980), 31–32.
9. Shirley M. Jackson, "Spanish American Literature for Today's Adolescents: The Afro-Hispanic Contribution," *Middle Atlantic Writer's Association Review* 1, no. 3 (1988): 16.
10. James J. Davis, "On Black Poetry in the Dominican Republic," *Afro-Hispanic Review* 1, no. 3 (1982): 29.
11. In addition to the studies I cite, see also Marvin Lewis, "Contemporary Afro-Dominican Poetry: The Example of Blas R. Jiménez, *College Language Association Journal* 34, no. 3 (1991): 301–16; and James Davis, "Ritmo poético, negritud y dominicanidad," *Revista iberoamericana* 142 (January–March 1988): 171–86.

Chapter Ten

1. Antonio Acosta Márquez, *Yo pienso aquí . . . donde estoy* (Medellín: Editorial Cascabel, 1977; Caracas: Editorial Trazos, 1981). Quotations taken from the second edition and cited in text as *Yo pienso.*
2. See Richard Jackson, "A Modern Black Everyman," *Black Literature and Humanism in Latin America* (Athens: University of Georgia Press, 1988), 56–60.
3. Laura Hidalgo Alzamora, *Décimas Esmeraldeñas* (Quito: Centro de Investigación y Cultura, 1982).
4. Juan García Salazar, "Black Poetry of Coastal Ecuador," *Grassroots Development: Journal of the Inter-American Foundation* 8, no. 1 (1984): 31–37.

5. Julio Antonio León, "Afro-Cuban Poetry: An Unpublished Treasure" *Americas* 29, no. 9 (1977): 28–37.

6. See Richard Jackson, "In the Beginning: Oral Literature and the 'True Black Experience,'" *Black Writers in Latin America* (Albuquerque: University of New Mexico Press, 1979), 16–24. Also see Richard Jackson, "The Path to Enlightenment," *Black Literature and Latin America: Contemporary Issues* (Washington, D.C.: Howard University Press, forthcoming).

7. Ian I. Smart, *Nicolás Guillén. Popular Poet of the Caribbean* (Columbia: University of Missouri Press, 1990), 9.

8. Laurence E. Prescott, *Candelario Obeso y la iniciación de la poesía negra en Colombia* (Bogotá: Instituto Caro y Cuervo, 1985).

9. Henry Richards and Teresa Cajiao Salas, *Asedios a la poesía de Nicomedes Santa Cruz* (Quito: Editora Andina, 1982).

10. Nicomedes Santa Cruz, *Décimas y poemas, antología* (Lima: Campodónico Ediciones, 1971), 16. Hereafter cited in text as *Décimas*.

11. Nicomedes Santa Cruz, *Ritmos negros del Perú* (Buenos Aires: Losada, 1971). Hereafter cited in text as *Ritmos*.

12. Marvin Lewis, *Afro-Hispanic Poetry, 1940–1980. From Slavery to "Negritud" in South American Verse* (Columbia: University of Missouri Press, 1983), 53. Hereafter cited in text as Lewis.

13. In a personal interview with Marvin Lewis, 8 June 1979 (Lewis 1983, 178); in the introduction to *Décimas* (15), and in Elena Poniatowska, "Habla el peruano Nicomedes Santa Cruz," *¡Siempre!,* 14 August 1974, 39–41, 70.

14. Marvin Lewis, *Ethnicity and Identity in Contemporary Afro-Venezuelan Literature. A Culturalist Approach* (Columbia: University of Missouri Press, 1992).

15. *Aloud. Voices from the Nuyorican Poets Cafe,* ed. Miguel Algarín and Bob Holman (New York: Henry Holt and Co., 1994). Hereafter cited in text as *Aloud.*

Chapter Eleven

1. Edward J. Mullen, "The Emergence of Afro-Hispanic Poetry: Some Notes on Canon Formation," *Hispanic Review* 56, no. 4 (1988): 435–53.

2. Howard Mancing, "A Consensus Canon of Hispanic Poetry," *Hispania* 69, no. 1 (1986): 53–81.

3. See Marvin Lewis, *Afro-Hispanic Poetry, 1940–1980. From Slavery to "Negritude" in South American Verse* (Columbia: University of Missouri Press, 1983).

4. See Michael Handelsman, "Ubicando la literatura afroecuatoriana en el contexto nacional: ¿Ilusión o realidad?" (paper presented at the Fourth Annual Hispanic Literature and Culture Conference, Southern Arkansas Univer-

sity, Magnolia, Arkansas, November 2, 1991. Also published in *Afro-Hispanic Review* 12, no. 1 (1993): 42–47. Hereafter cited in text as Handelsman.

    5. See Richard L. Jackson, "The Authenticity Question," *Black Literature and Humanism in Latin America* (Athens: University of Georgia Press, 1988), 1–19.

    6. D.P. Gallagher, *Modern Latin American Literature* (London: Oxford University Press, 1973), 84.

    7. Gordon Brotherston, "Vernacular American," in *Latin American Poetry: Origins and Presence* (Cambridge: Cambridge University Press, 1975), 7–26. Hereafter cited in text as Brotherston.

    8. Richard Jackson, "The Authenticity Question Revisited," *Black Literature and Latin America: Contemporary Issues* (Washington, D.C.: Howard University Press, forthcoming).

    9. Keith Ellis, *Cuba's Nicolás Guillén: Poetry and Ideology* (Toronto: University of Toronto Press, 1983), 193.

    10. René de Costa, *The Poetry of Pablo Neruda* (Cambridge: Harvard University Press, 1979), 105.

    11. Guillermo Araya, "El Canto general de Neruda: poema épico-lírico," *Revista de crítica literaria latinoamericana* 13, nos. 7–8 (1978): 134.

    12. Pablo Neruda, *Confieso que he vivido* (Buenos Aires: Losada, 1976), 235.

Selected Bibliography

PRIMARY SOURCES

Acosta Márquez, Antonio. *Yo pienso aquí donde . . . estoy*. Medellín: Editorial Cascabel, 1977. A second edition, published by Editorial Trazos in Caracas in 1981, contains several new poems.

"Afro-Uruguayan Poetry." *Afro-Hispanic Review* 12, no. 2 (1993): 37–47. Includes selections from early to contemporary Afro-Uruguayan poets.

Artel, Jorge. *Tambores en la noche*. Cartagena: Ediciones Bolívar, 1940. One of the pioneering books of Black Hispanic poetry. A second edition, published by Ediciones de la Universidad de Guanajuato in 1955, contains several new poems. A third edition was published in Bogotá in 1986 by Plaza y Janés.

Barrios, Pilar. *Piel negra. Poesías (1917–1947)*. Montevideo: Nuestra Raza, 1947. Reprint, Nendeln: Kraus, 1970. Both this book, Barrios's first, and his other two, *Mis cantos* (1949) and *Campo afuera* (1959), are available in the Kraus reprint.

Britos Serrat, Alberto ed. *Antología de poetas uruguayos*. Montevideo: Ediciones Mundo Afro, 1991. Gives exposure to new-generation Black poets in Uruguay. Useful despite a controversial introduction.

Duncan, Quince. *Los cuatro espejos*. San José: Editorial Costa Rica, 1973. The first novel by Duncan that brought his name to the wider reading public.

———. *Kimbo*. San José: Editorial Costa Rica, 1990. Duncan's most recent novel and, according to the novelist, his best yet.

Estupiñán Bass, Nelson. *El último río*. Quito: Casa de la Cultura Ecuatoriana, 1966. The first edition of this novel, considered to be Estupiñán Bass's most controversial.

———. *El último río*. 2d ed. Quito: Casa de la Cultura Económica, 1980. This second edition contains some material deleted from the first edition.

———. *Pastrana's Last River*. Trans. Ian Smart. Washington, D.C.: Afro-Hispanic Institute, 1993. Smart translates from the first edition.

Guillén, Nicolás. *The Daily Daily*. Trans. Vera Kutzinski. Berkeley: University of California Press, 1989. A translation of *El diario que a diario*, which Kutzinski considers to be Guillén's most ambitious poetic project.

———. *Páginas vueltas. Memorias*. Havana: Ediciones Unión, 1982. Guillén's autobiographical memoirs.

———. *Obra poética 1958–1972*. 2 vols. Havana: Editorial Arte y Literatura, 1974. The first comprehensive edition of Guillén's poetry. This valuable compilation, edited by Angel Augier, includes his earliest poems.

Hernández, Gaspar Octavio. *Obras selectas.* Ed. Octavio Augusto Hernández. Panama: Imprenta Nacional, 1966. A large volume of 589 pages, complete with a biographical introduction and a bibliography of works by and about "The Black Swan," as Hernández was known. Contains Hernández's poem "Ergo sum."

James, Norberto. *Sobre la Marcha.* In *Hago constar (poemas—1969–1972).* Santo Domingo: Editora Taller, 1983: 9–49. Contains his prize-winning poem "Los inmigrantes."

Jiménez, Blas R. *Aquí . . . otro español.* Santo Domingo: Editorial Incoco, 1980.

———. *Caribe africano en despertar.* Santo Domingo: Ediciones Nuevas Rutas, 1984.

———. *Exigencias de un cimarrón (en sueños).* Santo Domingo: Editora Taller, 1987.

Maloney, Gerardo. *Juega vivo.* Panama: Ediciones Formato Dieciseis, 1984.

Manzano, Juan Francisco. *Autobiografía de un esclavo.* Ed. Ivan A. Schulman. Madrid: Ediciones Guadarrama, 1975. A modernized version based on José L. Franco, *Autobiografía, cartas y versos de Juan Francisco Manzano* (Havana: Municipio de La Habana, 1937). The English versions of Manzano's "Mis treinta años" and the *Autobiografía,* translated and published by R.R. Madden in 1840, are contained in *The Life and Times of a Cuban Slave. Juan Francisco Manzano 1797–1854,* ed. Edward J. Mullen (Hamden, CT: Archon Books, 1981).

Morejón, Nancy. "Amo a mi amo." *Octubre imprescindible.* Havana: Ediciones Unión, 1982, 45–47.

———. "Mujer negra." *Parajes de una época.* Havana: Editorial Letras Cubanas, 1979, 18–20. First published in 1975 in *Casa de las Américas* 15, no. 88 (1975): 19–20.

———. *Where the Island Sleeps Like a Wing.* Trans. Kathleen Weaver. San Francisco: The Black Scholar Press, 1985. Contains a good cross section of Morejón's poems.

Morúa Delgado, Martín. *Obras completas.* Havana: Impresores Nosotros, 1957. 5 vols. The first two volumes contain Morúa Delgado's novels *Sofía* (1891) and *La familia Unzúazu* (1901).

Obeso, Candelario. *Cantos populares de mi tierra.* Bogotá: Biblioteca Popular de Cultura Colombiana, 1950. Also contains *Lectura para ti* and *Lucha de la vida.*

Ortiz, Adalberto. *Juyungo.* Barcelona: Seix Barral, 1976. The most popular and available edition of the 1943 original.

———. *Juyungo.* Trans. Susan Hill and Jonathan Titler. Washington, D.C.: Three Continents Press, 1982. This translation of *Juyungo* was the first Black Hispanic novel to appear in English.

Palacios, Arnoldo. *Las estrellas son negras.* Bogotá: Editorial Iqueima, 1949; Bogotá: Editorial Revista Colombiana, 1971. Has been considered Colombia's most naturalistic novel.

Santa Cruz, Nicomedes. *Ritmos negros del Perú*. Buenos Aires: Losada, 1971. This edition, which had a second printing in 1973, draws from earlier volumes. Also contains some poems not previously published. A much larger collection of his works is available in the collection *Décimas y poemas, antología* (Lima: Campodónico Ediciones, 1971).

Sojo, Juan Pablo. *Nochebuena negra*. Caracas: Editorial General Rafael Urdaneta, 1943; Caracas: Monte Avila Editores, 1972.

Truque, Carlos Arturo. "Mi testimonio." *Afro-Hispanic Review* 1, no. 1 (1982): 17–22. Published here for the first time and translated ("My Testimony") by June M. Legge.

Valdés, Gabriel de la Concepción (Plácido). *Los poemas más representativos de Plácido (Edición crítica)*. Ed. Frederick S. Stimson and Humberto E. Robles. Chapel Hill, NC: Estudios de Hispanófila, 1976. Modernized selections based on the Sebastián Alfredo Morales edition of 1886. Groups poems thematically and includes in one section Plácido's poems associated with his death.

Wilson, Carlos Guillermo (Cubena). *Chombo*. Miami: Ediciones Universal, 1981. The first volume of a proposed trilogy.

———. *Los nietos de Felicidad Dolores*. Miami: Ediciones Universal, 1990. The second volume of the proposed trilogy.

Zapata Olivella, Manuel. *Chambacú: Black Slum*. Trans. Jonathan Tittler. Pittsburgh: Latin American Literary Review Press, 1989. Tittler does not translate from the original 1963 edition but from a later, abridged one.

———. *Chambacú, corral de negros*. Ed. José Luis Diaz Granados. Bogota: Rei Andes, 1990. An excellent scholastic edition. Based on the original 1963 version but uses the title associated with later editions.

———. *Changó, el gran putas*. Bogotá: Rei Andes, 1992. This is the most recent edition.

———. *Corral de negros*. Havana: Casa de las Américas, 1963. This is the original edition, published in Cuba a year after winning a literary award in that country.

———. *He visto la noche*. Bogotá: Editorial Andes, 1953; Medellín: Editorial Bedout, 1969, 1974.

———. *¡Levántate mulato!* Bogotá: Rei Andes, 1990. This work was first published in French as *Lève toi mulâtre!* (Paris: Payot, 1987).

SECONDARY SOURCES

Bibliographies

Jackson, Richard. *The Afro-Spanish American Author: An Annotated Bibliography of Criticism*. New York: Garland Publishing Co., 1980. The first of an ongoing series of annotated bibliographies of criticism on Black Hispanic writers. Comprehensive.

———. *The Afro-Spanish American Author II: The 1980s: An Annotated Bibliography of Recent Criticism.* West Cornwall, CT: Locust Hill Press, 1989. The second in the series, covering criticism that appeared in the 1980s, including newer Black Hispanic authors who gained prominence during that decade.

Books

Augier, Angel. *Nicolás Guillén. Estudio biográfico-crítico.* Havana: Ediciones Union, 1984. Indispensable biography of Guillén with interpretations of his poetry. This edition brings to date the first edition published in 1962 in two volumes and in 1965 as one.

Birmingham-Pokorny, Elba, ed. *Denouncement and Reaffirmation of the Afro-Hispanic Identity in Carlos Guillermo Wilson's Work.* Miami: Ediciones Universal, 1993. Contains several articles on Wilson's work, both early and most recent. Also contains an interview with the author.

Calcagno, Francisco. *Poetas de color (Plácido, Manzano, Rodríguez, Echemendía, Silveira, Medina).* 4th ed. Havana: Imprenta Mercantil de los Herederos de Santiago, 1887. This first study of Black poets who wrote in Spanish largely details the life and works of Manzano and Plácido.

Captain-Hidalgo, Yvonne. *The Culture of Fiction in the Works of Manuel Zapata Olivella.* Columbia: University of Missouri Press, 1994. The first comprehensive study in English of Zapata Olivella's works.

Caraballo, Vicente. *El negro Obeso. (Candelario). Apuntes biográficos y escritos varios.* Bogotá: Editorial A.B.C., 1943. Believed Obeso deserved wider exposure and wrote this work to try to make it happen.

Chrisman, Robert, ed. "Langston Hughes: Six Letters to Nicolás Guillén." Trans. Carmen Alegría. *The Black Scholar* 16, no. 4 (1985): 54–60. These letters outline what was one of the longest and most significant literary friendships of the twentieth century.

deCosta, Miriam, ed. *Blacks in Hispanic Literature: Critical Essays.* Port Washington, NY: Kennikat Press, 1977. The first collection ever of critical essays "by a group of distinguished black scholars" on Black Hispanic literature.

Coulthard, G.R. *Race and Colour in Caribbean Literature.* London: Oxford University Press, 1962. Perhaps the most influential early book on this subject. First published in 1958 by the Escuela de Estudios Hispano-Americanos de Sevilla, under the title *Raza y color en la literatura antillana.*

Ellis, Keith. *Cuba's Nicolás Guillén. Poetry and Ideology.* Toronto: University of Toronto Press, 1983. A comprehensive analysis of Guillén's poetry. Combines literary history and close textual analysis.

Finn, Julio. *Voices of Negritude.* London: Quartet Books, 1988. One of the few general books that gives extensive coverage to Afro-Hispanism.

Foster, David William. *Alternate Voices in the Contemporary Latin American Narrative.* Columbia: University of Missouri Press, 1985. Important because it gives legitimacy to works outside the mainstream. Takes a more comprehensive approach to Latin American fiction and considers works on the basis of criteria other than their international stature or reliance on foreign models.

Friol, Roberto. *Suite para Juan Francisco Manzano.* Havana: Editorial Arte y Literatura, 1977. An excellent compilation of documentation on and opinion about Manzano's life and works.

Homenaje a Carlos Arturo Truque. Special issue of *Afro-Hispanic Review* [6, no. 3 (1987)]. Contains several informative articles about Truque's life and works.

Horrego Estuch, Leopoldo. *Martín Morúa Delgado. Vida y mensaje.* Havana: Comisión Nacional del Centenario de Martín Morúa Delgado, 1959. Reviews the author's life and works and makes a good comparison between Morúa Delgado's novel *Sofía* and Cirilo Villaverde's *Cecilia Valdés.*

Jackson, Richard. *The Black Image in Latin American Literature.* Albuquerque: University of New Mexico Press, 1976. Largely devoted to non-Black writers associated, for the most part, with Black themes.

———. *Black Literature and Humanism in Latin America.* Athens: University of Georgia Press, 1988. Considers Black Hispanic writers to be models expressing representative Latin American themes.

———. *Black Literature and Latin America: Contemporary Issues.* Washington, D.C.: Howard University Press. Forthcoming. Discusses some of the major issues relevant to Afro-Hispanism.

———. *Black Writers and Latin America: Cross-Cultural Affinities.* Washington: Howard University Press. Forthcoming. Explores contacts, influences, and cross-cultural interests and experiences.

———. *Black Writers in Latin America.* Albuquerque: University of New Mexico Press, 1979. Establishes major periods and authors. Organized chronologically.

Jahn, Janheinz. *A History of Neo-African Literature.* Trans. Oliver Coburn and Ursula Lehrburger. London: Faber and Faber, Ltd., 1968. A major work on Black literature in the New World.

Kubayanda, J.B. *The Poet's Africa: Africanness in the Poetry of Nicolás Guillén and Aimé Césaire.* New York: Greenwood Press, 1990. Extensive example of Kubayanda's linguistic and Africanist approach to Guillén's poetry.

Kutzinski, Vera. *Against the American Grain: Myth and History in William Carlos Williams, Jay Wright, and Nicolás Guillén.* Baltimore: The Johns Hopkins University Press, 1987. Her first major publication on Guillén. Focuses specifically on *El diario que a diario,* which she considers an innovative book that, poetically speaking, contains "all of Guillén."

————, ed. *Nicolás Guillén: A Special Issue* [*Callaloo* 10, no. 2 (1987)]. Includes "advanced" studies on Guillén's poetry and an interview with the poet himself, in conversation with Laurence Prescott.

————. *Sugar's Secrets: Race and the Erotics of Cuban Nationalism.* Charlottesville: University Press of Virginia, 1993. Her new book, controversial in part because of its feminist approach to Guillén's poetry.

Lewis, Marvin A. *Afro-Hispanic Poetry, 1940–1980. From Slavery to "Negritud" in South American Verse.* Columbia: University of Missouri Press, 1983. A nice complement to genre studies that overlook the poets Lewis studies.

————. *Ethnicity and Identity in Contemporary Afro-Venezuelan Literature. A Culturalist Approach.* Columbia: University of Missouri Press, 1992. Important study that shows how two Black writers in Venezuela fought each in his own time against invisibility.

————. *Treading the Ebony Path: Ideology and Violence in Contemporary Afro-Colombian Prose Fiction.* Columbia: University of Missouri Press, 1987. Examines the prose fiction of Arnoldo Palacios, Carlos A. Truque, Jorge Artel, Juan Zapata Olivella, and Manuel Zapata Olivella.

Luis, William. *Literary Bondage: Slavery in Cuban Narrative.* Austin: University of Texas Press, 1990. Contains excellent section on Manzano.

————, ed. *Voices from Under: Black Narrative in Latin America and the Caribbean.* Westport, CT: Greenwood Press, 1984. A useful reference collection of several essays. Includes one on Manzano and another on Adalberto Ortiz's *Juyungo.*

Martínez-Echazábal, Lourdes. *Para una semiótica de la mulatez.* Madrid: Ediciones José Porrúa Turanzas, 1990. Deemphasizes Blackness in her interpretations.

Moore, Carlos. *Castro, the Blacks and Africa.* Berkeley: University of California Press, 1989. The anti-Castro, pro-Black volume that probably gave rise to the Pérez Sarduy/Stubbs anthology listed below.

Morejón, Nancy, ed. *Recopilación de textos sobre Nicolás Guillén.* Havana: Casa de las Americas, 1974. Includes Morejón's collage of conversations with Guillén.

Mullen, Edward, ed. *Nancy Morejón. A Special Issue* [*Afro-Hispanic Review* 15, no. 1 (1996)]. Articles included are the result of a symposium held in 1995 at the University of Missouri-Columbia, with Nancy Morejón in attendance.

Pérez Sarduy, Pedro, and Jean Stubbs, eds. *AfroCuba: An Anthology of Cuban Writing on Race, Politics and Culture.* Melbourne: Ocean Press, 1993. A curious volume because for the most part it excludes Manzano, Morejón, and Guillén.

Prescott, Laurence. *Candelario Obeso y la iniciación de la poesía negra en Colombia.* Bogotá: Instituto Caro y Cuervo, 1985. Detailed study of *Cantos populares de mi tierra,* Obeso's best-known work.

Richards, Henry J., and Teresa C. Salas. *Asedios a la poesía de Nicomedes Santa Cruz*. Quito: Editora Andina, 1982. Includes previously published and new work.

———. *La jornada novelística de Nelson Estupiñán Bass: búsqueda de la perfección*. Quito: Editorial El Cornejo, 1989. Studies all of Estupiñán Bass's novels up to that date.

Rivas, Mercedes. *Literatura y esclavitud en la novela cubana del siglo XIX*. Sevilla: Escuela de Estudios Hispano-Americanos de Sevilla, 1990. Provides good historical background to the literature.

Sardinha, Dennis. *The Poetry of Nicolás Guillén. An Introduction*. London: New Books Ltd., 1970. Includes a translation of an interview with the poet held in 1972.

Smart, Ian. *Central American Writers of West Indian Origin: A New Hispanic Literature*. Washington D.C.: Three Continents Press, 1984. Groundbreaking study of this new Hispanic literature.

———. *Nicolás Guillén: Popular Poet of the Caribbean*. Columbia: University of Missouri Press, 1990. Relates Guillén's poetry to Caribbean poetics.

Sojo, Juan Pablo. *Temas y apuntes afro-venezolanos*. Caracas: Tip. La Nación, 1943.

Stimson, Frederick S. *Cuba's Romantic Poet. The Story of Plácido*. Chapel Hill: University of North Carolina Press, 1964. Tries to draw emphasis away from the North American interest in the sensational aspects of the Plácido story.

White, Clement A. *Decoding the Word: Nicolás Guillén as Maker and Debunker of Myth*. Miami: Ediciones Universal, 1993. This most recent book on Guillén rejects what its author considers to be all of the misguided assumptions about the poet that have gone before.

Williams, Lorna. *The Representation of Slavery in Cuban Fiction*. Columbia: University of Missouri Press, 1994. The most recent and one of the most extensive treatments of this subject.

Articles

Bolden, Millicent A. "Conversación entre Nelson Estupiñán Bass y Millicent A. Bolden." *Afro-Hispanic Review* 7, no. 3 (1989): 14–16. Discusses several topics, among them his many literary activities.

Captain, Yvonne. "Conversación con el doctor Manuel Zapata Olivella." *Afro-Hispanic Review* 4, no. 1 (1985): 26–32. Talks at length about his *Changó, el gran putas* and its epic quality.

———. "Writing for the Future: Afro-Hispanism in a Global, Critical Context." *Afro-Hispanic Review* 13, no. 1 (1994): 3–8. Calls for new directions in Afro-Hispanic criticism but cautions against interventions by nonspecialist interlopers.

Cyrus, Stanley. "Ethnic Ambivalence and Afro-Hispanic Novelists." *Afro-Hispanic Review* 1, no. 1 (1982): 29–32. Important for its exploration of reasons why some authors are ambivalent and for pointing out Carlos A. Truque's scathing denunciations on "elitist and whitish-oriented" attitudes among publishers and critics that sometimes influence writers.

Davis, James J. "Entrevista con el dominicano Norberto James Rawlings." *Afro-Hispanic Review* 6, no. 2 (1987): 16–18. Talks of his family, educational background, and influences.

———. "On Black poetry in the Dominican Republic." *Afro-Hispanic Review* 1, no. 3 (1982): 27–30. General overview but highlights Black Dominican writers.

Davis-Lett, Stephanie. "Blacks and Criollism: A Curious Relationship." *College Language Association Journal* 24, no. 2 (1980): 131–49. One of the first studies of this relationship between the Black image and national culture and identity.

Ellis, Keith. "Images of Black People in the Poetry of Nicolás Guillén." *Afro-Hispanic Review* 7, nos. 1–3 (1988): 19–22. Focuses on the true nature of Guillén's work while criticizing some who miss the point.

———. "Nicolás Guillén. Interview with Keith Ellis." *Jamaican Journal* 7, nos. 1–2 (1973): 17–19. One of the interviews in which Guillén says negritude poems in Cuba today would be considered racist.

Escrivá-Carnicer, Angela. "Crossing the Last River: The Search for Identity in Nelson Estupiñán Bass's *El último río*." *Diáspora* 1 (1991): 52–62. A good analysis of the relationship between José Pastrana and Ana Mercedes.

Gómez, Gilberto, and Raymond L. Williams. "Interview with Manuel Zapata Olivella." *Hispania* 67, no. 4 (1984): 657–58. Discusses his ambitious technique in *Changó, el gran putas* and that novel's Black perspective.

Green-Williams, Claudette Rose. "Re-Writing the History of the Afro-Cuban Woman: Nancy Morejón's 'Mujer negra.' " *Afro-Hispanic Review* 7, no. 3 (1989): 17–13. One of the earlier studies of this poem.

Handelsman, Michael, "Ubicando la literatura afroecuatoriana en el contexto nacional: ¿Ilusión o realidad? *Afro-Hispanic Review* 12, no. 1 (1993): 42–47. Recognizes the importance, both to the authors themselves and to their readers, of literature on the Black experience written by Blacks.

Howe, Linda. "Nancy Morejón's 'Mujer negra': Rereading Afrocentric Hermeneutics, Rewriting Gender." *The Journal of Afro-Latin American Studies and Literatures* 1, no. 1 (1993–1994): 95–107. A rereading, as the title indicates—and a good one—of Morejón's major poem.

Jackson, Shirley M. "Spanish American Literature for Today's Adolescents: the Afro-Hispanic Contribution." *Middle Atlantic Writer's Association Review* 1, no. 3 (1988): 15–18. Prizes Black Hispanic literature for the positive values it represents. Makes the same good points in "The Special Gift of Literature," *Monographic Review/Revista monográfica* (1985): 83–89.

James, Norberto. "First Person Singular?" In *Being America: Essays on Art, Literature and Identity from Latin America,* edited by Rachel Weiss with Alan West, 51–58. Fredonia, NY: White Pine Press, 1991. Informative introduction to the poet as told by himself.

Kubayanda, J.B. "Hispanic Humanism and Nineteenth-Century Cuban Blacks: An Historico-Literary Perspective." *Plantation Society* 1, no. 3 (1981): 343–63. Argues that nineteenth-century Black slavery certainly was not a humanizing experience.

———. "Minority Discourse and the African Collective: Some Examples from Latin American and Caribbean Literature." *Cultural Critique* 6 (Spring 1987): 113–30. Laments the critical neglect of Black literature in Latin America.

Larrier, Renée. "Racism in the United States: An Issue in Caribbean Studies." *Journal of Caribbean Studies* 2, no. 1 (1981): 51–71. Guillén and Morejón stand foremost on this theme among the poets who write in Spanish.

Lewis, Marvin. "Contemporary Afro-Dominican Poetry: The Example of Blas R. Jiménez." *College Language Association Journal* 34, no. 3 (1991): 301–16. A good introduction to Jiménez's poetry.

Luis, William. "Autobiografía del esclavo Juan Francisco Manzano: versión de Suárez y Romero." In *Memorias del 26 Congreso del Instituto Internacional de Literatura Iberoamericana,* edited by Raquel Chang-Rodríguez and Gabriella de Beer. Hanover: Ediciones del Norte, 1989. Sheds light on the multiple versions of Manzano's *Autobiografía.*

McElroy, Onyria Herrera. "Martín Morúa Delgado, precursor del afro-cubanismo." *Afro-Hispanic Review* 11, no. 1 (1983): 19–24. A fine article that consolidates Morúa Delgado's reputation as a precursor of Afro-Cubanism.

Molloy, Sylvia. "From Serf to Self: The Autobiography of Juan Francisco Manzano." *Modern Language Notes. Hispanic Issue* 104. no. 2 (1989): 393–417. Excellent study of Manzano and his autobiography.

Mullen, Edward J. "Afro-Hispanic and Afro-American Literary Historiography: Comments on Generational Shifts." *College Language Association Journal* 38, no. 4 (1995): 371–89. Discussion covers much of the work in Black Hispanic criticism, including some of the pioneering studies of Martha Cobb.

———. "The Emergence of Afro-Hispanic Poetry: Some Notes on Canon Formation." *Hispanic Review* 56, no. 4 (1988): 435–53. Discusses the evolution of this poetry, especially as represented in anthologies.

———. "Some Early Readings of *Motivos de son.*" *Romance Notes* 39, no. 2 (1992): 221–30. Discusses the early critical reaction to these poems.

Newman, Ronna Smith. "Conversación con Adalberto Ortiz." *Cultura* (Quito), May–August 1983: 189–210. In this follow-up to her dissertation on Ortiz, Newman reports on the authors's views on his writing habits, background, recent works, and current interests.

Prescott, Laurence. "A Conversation with Nicolás Guillén." *Nicolás Guillén: A Special Issue* [*Callaloo* 10, no. 2 (1987)]: 352–54.

Richards, Henry. "Entrevista con Nelson Estupiñán Bass." *Afro-Hispanic Review* 2, no. 1 (1983): 29–30. Richards's first of several interviews with Estupiñán Bass is notable in part because the Ecuadorian author states his belief that he is more esteemed abroad than at home.

———. "Narrative Strategies in Nelson Estupiñán Bass's *El último río*." *Afro-Hispanic Review* 1, no. 1 (1982): 11–15. Careful analysis of Estupiñán Bass's art.

———. "Nelson Estupiñán Bass on *El último río*." *Afro-Hispanic Review* 10, no. 1 (1991): 21–23. Estupiñán Bass responds to questions put to him in writing by students.

Rodríguez, Rafael. "Nancy Morejón en su Habana." *Areito* 8, no. 32 (1983): 23–25. Important interview in which Morejón talks at length about "Mujer negra."

Sims, Edna. " 'Is There a Battle of the Sexes in *El último río?*' A Comparative Study." *Middle Atlantic Writers Association Review* 3, no. 1 (1988): 19–22. Addresses one of the central issues raised in the novel.

Smart, Ian. "*Changó, El Gran Putas* as Liberation Literature." *College Language Association Journal* 35, no. 1 (1991): 15–30. Considers the novel to be a work of "fighting literature" in the Fanonian sense.

———. "The Literary World of Quince Duncan: An Interview." *College Language Association Journal* 28, no. 3 (1985): 281–98. Wide-ranging conversation. Includes discussions of Duncan's background, influences, and craft as a writer.

———. "Popular Black Intellectualism in Gerardo Maloney's *Juega vivo*." *Afro-Hispanic Review* 5, nos. 1–3 (1986): 43–47. One of the first studies on Maloney's poetry.

Socarrás, José Francisco. "En el centenario de Candelario Obeso." *Boletín de la Academia Colombiana* 150 (October–December 1985): 245–61. Good review of Obeso's life and accomplishments. Considers him a precursor of Jorge Artel and Nicolás Guillén.

Index

INDEX

The Author

Richard Jackson is professor of Spanish American literature at Carleton University in Ottawa, Canada. He is the author of numerous publications on Black Hispanic writers, including *The Black Image in Latin American Literature* (Albuquerque: University of New Mexico Press, 1976), *Black Writers in Latin America* (Albuquerque: University of New Mexico Press, 1979), *Black Literature and Humanism in Latin America* (Athens: University of Georgia Press, 1988), *Black Writers and Latin America: Cross-Cultural Affinities* (Washington, D.C.: Howard University Press, forthcoming), and *Black Literature and Latin America: Contemporary Issues* (Washington, D.C.: Howard University Press, forthcoming). In 1994 he was named a Fellow of the Royal Society of Canada.

The Editor

David William Foster is Regents' Professor of Spanish and Director of Spanish Graduate Studies at Arizona State University, where he also chairs the Publications Committee of the Center for Latin American Studies. He is known for his extensive contributions in the field of Latin American literary bibliography and reference works. In addition, he has published numerous monographs on Latin American literature, with emphasis on theater and narrative, the most recent of which is *Violence in Argentine Literature: Cultural Responses to Tyranny* (University of Missouri Press, 1995).